GUIDE TO
TROLLEY MODEL BUILDING

An introduction to an
interesting phase of
Model Building for
all gauges.

Prepared by the Traction Guild.
Edited by W. K. Walthers with
the assistance of R. M. Wagner.

September 1958

WILDSIDE PRESS
COVER PHOTO BY MILWAUKEE SENTINEL

TABLE OF CONTENTS

GUIDE TO
TROLLEY MODEL BUILDING

An introduction to an
interesting phase of
Model Building for
all gauges.

Prepared by the Traction Guild.
Edited by W. K. Walthers with
the assistance of R. M. Wagner.

September 1958

WILDSIDE PRESS
COVER PHOTO BY MILWAUKEE SENTINEL

PARTIAL LIST OF NMRA STANDARD
DIMENSIONS FOR USE ON MODEL TRACTION LINES

GAUGE

	O	S	OO	HO
Track Width—inside to inside of rail heads	1.250"	0.875"	0.750"	0.650"
Inside of outer running rail to center of outside third rail	11/16"	7/16"	25/64"	5/16"
Height of outside third rail above running rail	1/8"	3/32"	5/64"	1/16"
Number of Trolley Wire	24	26-30	26-30	26-30
Trolley Wire Heights from rail	4 3/4"-5 1/2"	3 9/16"-4 1/8"	2 7/8"-3 15/16"	2 1/2"-3"
Min. centers dbl. track—straight	4"	2 3/4"	2 1/4"	2"
Min. centers dbl. track 10" radius	5"-6 1/2"	8"r 3 3/4"-4 7/8"	7"r 2 3/4"-3 1/8"	6"r 2 1/2"-2 7/8"
Min. centers dbl. track 36" radius	5"	27"r 3 3/4"	20"r 2 3/4"	18"r 2 1/2"
Min. centers dbl. track 40" radius	4 1/2"	30"r 3 3/8"	22"r 2 1/2"	20"r 2 1/4"
Min. centers dbl. track 44" radius	4 1/4"	33"r 3 1/8"	25"r 2 3/8"	22"r 2 1/8"
Center line of track to pole—straight track	1 1/2"	1 1/8"	15/16"	13/16"
Center line of track to pole—main-line curves	1 3/4"	1 1/2"	1 19/32"	1 1/8"

Reproduced by permission of National Model Railroad Association, Inc.

For complete set of standards as adopted and published by the NMRA it is recommended that the model traction fan join the aforementioned organization.

For further details write the Association.

FIG. 1 NMRA STANDARDS FOR USE ON MODEL TRACTION LINES.

Chapter 1

WHY BUILD A MODEL TROLLEY LINE?

Why build a model of a trolley line? With so many steam, diesel and electric railroads to choose for a prototype, and with such a variety of motive power, freight and passenger cars to model, why should one choose a trolley line? It would seem that such a choice would leave the hobbyist a very restricted field in which to carry out any "empire building" ambitions. There are some excellent reasons in favor of model trolley lines which we would like to present as an introductory chapter to this Guide.

First of all, the trolley line has just as much to fascinate the model builder as any other type of railroad. Trolleys have played an important role in the development of transportation in this country and anyone with a desire to reproduce an interesting part of this development will find a trolley line an engaging and challenging project. There is room for research, as well as building, and for the realist or exhibitionist there is an opportunity to portray a scene in the passing parade of "wheels 'a rolling". This is particularly true with trolleys as they are slowly giving up their ghost to other forms of transportation.

For the man who desires to make a modest approach to a miniature railroad system the trolley line offers the simplest program. One trolley car, a short stretch of track and a minimum of electrical equipment provides an operating system. It does not require a large amount of planning before starting and the results of ones work are soon put in service. For one who would like to take up the hobby of model railroading, but has qualms about his ability to build or apply himself to any constructional work, here is a good field in which to experiment without getting started on something that does not seem to have an end. Much can be done with a minimum expenditure of time and money.

Where space is at a premium and a railroad system is either impossible or if carried out at all would be restricted, a trolley line is ideal. A shelf only six inches wide running along one or two sides of a basement wall, attic or even spare room will do. No wide platforms are necessary on which to build loops or circles as the trolley line can operate on a "point-to-point" track starting at one end, running to the other end of the line and then running back without even turning the car around. No large radii curves are needed as the trolley car goes round a 35' curve (9" radius in O gauge 7" for S and 5" in HO), requires no "yards" for car storage or space taking terminals and round houses.

For those who have started with a toy railroad, the trolley line offers a place for your toy track when converting your system to scale. Trolley cars with large flanged wheels suitable for running on tin-plate track are available. The small radii of the toy track is more than ample for trolley line service. Here then is a way to use something that you do not like to discard yet often proves a stumbling block when making up your mind to transfer from toy to scale equipment. A trolley line can always be fitted into a scale layout, for trolley lines and railroad tracks often run on parallel right of ways.

What you build for a trolley line is never lost should you later decide to enlarge your system to include steam or electric prototype equipment. Many a trolley line has grown up into an interurban system and sometimes even into a class 1 railroad. The track you build will always prove useful again on another type of road and should you require large curves, the old ones can be relaid if no longer usable. One must always keep in mind that whatever is done today must either grow or perish for that seems to be one of the basic laws of progress.

Just what is included in the classification "Trolley" line? We might define a trolley line as a method of wheeled transportation using cars which get their power from an overhead wire by means of a "trolley". The word "trolley" is defined by Webster as "a grooved metal wheel for rolling in contact with an electric conductor to convey electric energy to a motor car". We usually think of a trolley car as a "street" car traveling within the limits of a city.

Usually such cars operate in single units and occasionally in pairs. Sometimes the two cars in a pair have three trucks between them the center one serving as a pivot or articulation point. City cars, are of many varieties including the safety car nicknamed "Birney" after its designer, the high speed streamlined car known as the "PCC" car (so named because its design was chosen and standardized by a group of street car company presidents after a series of conferences - Presidents Conference Car), as well as all the older types still in service in many cities.

Operating also on a trolley is the Interurban car which is but an extended city line to join several near by cities and villages. Cars are somewhat longer than city cars and may be run singly or in groups depending on the traffic require-

ments of the line. Cars equipped with motors are known as power cars and those without power equipment as trailers. Interurban car types include many of the same kind of cars used in railroad passenger service such as coaches, combines (combination of coach and baggage), diners, parlor and observation cars. Some lines having longer runs also had sleeping cars. All of these are essentially "trolley" lines because they use the over head trolley wire for power.

There are interurban lines that use a "catenary" overhead wire with pantagraphs instead of trolley poles for power pick-up. While these should not be included as trolley lines because technically speaking they are not, we will however include all types of cars that have the appearance of trolley cars (or look like railroad passenger cars) because they all fit into the same kind of model building program and it is only a simple step from one to the next. Perhaps we should have called this book a Guide to Traction Systems, because this term fits all the types we shall mention. The term "trolley", however, has a little more romance connected with it.

Next in development we mention the Multiple-Unit car. This is the type used by railroads such as the New York Central, New Haven, Long Island and others in their suburb-

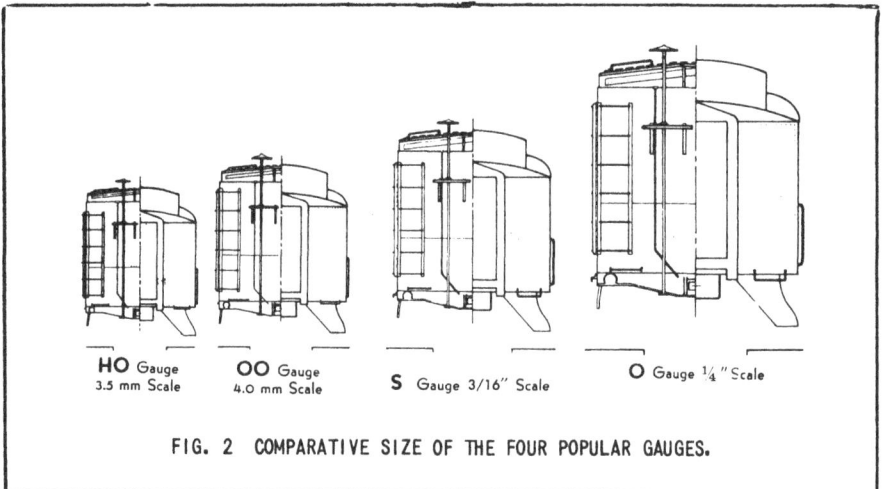

FIG. 2 COMPARATIVE SIZE OF THE FOUR POPULAR GAUGES.

HO Gauge 3.5 mm Scale   OO Gauge 4.0 mm Scale   S Gauge 3/16" Scale   O Gauge ¼" Scale

an passenger service. In the multiple unit language each car is a power car but so wired that all cars are controlled in multiple from a control cab in any car. In other respects this type is very much the same as interurban cars. Some in this class are as long as passenger cars. In the case of the NYC Power is taken from a third rail but the New Haven, Pennsylvania, Illinois Central and others use the overhead wire with pantagraph pick-ups.

Many of the interurban lines also have freight service and have locomotives rather than powerized cars for hauling the freight cars. Some lines use specially built cars as power units. It all depends on the length of train hauled and the extent of the roads freight service. Then there is the steeple cab type of switching locomotive used in making up freight trains and doing road repair work. Many electric traction lines have special types of cars not found on the larger road.

So, when you build a trolley line, you still have a wide choice of equipment with all the opportunity to expand. At the same time you may restrict your efforts to a small city system and yet have an operating system that is just as complete as a larger one would be. This great variety is one of the things that makes model transportation such an interesting hobby. We will turn now to outlining a program which will enable us to start small, experiment and expand as much as desired. Starting out

with the simplest form will also give you a nucleus which will serve to allow for operations while planning extensions.

Before Starting to Outline a project, let's cover a few fundamentals. Assuming that you are a stranger to model railroading, a few generalities should be covered. If you do not find all your questions answered herein we suggest the perusal of a book on model railroading in general. We can not very well go into complete detail on every phase of a hobby that has so many angles and approaches.

When you model to scale you build a miniature reproduction to dimensions which are in proportion or ratio to the actual dimensions of the prototype. What is called the "scale" is the ratio factor of the real to model dimensions. Thus when we say "1/4 inch scale" we mean that each foot in actual dimensions is reduced to 1/4". This is a ratio of 1:48. In model language we also speak of "gauge". This is just another way of indicating scale or ratio. "O" gauge is the same as 1/4" scale. Other gauges and scales are "S" (3/16" to the foot), "HO", (approximately 1/8" to the foot or actually 55% of O gauge), and others. The basic railroad dimensions reduced to the different scale figures are shown in the chart on the inside cover.

The first thing you do is to decide on the gauge or scale you are going to follow. It is not up to the writer to recommend any particular scale as best because he

Old style interurban car with wood sides and arch windows. For plans see Fig. 87.

wants to be unbiased and not pre-
judiced in any way. Your choice
will depend on the following fac-
tors: size of space available,
amount of detail you wish to incor-
porate, your desire for scenic ef-
fects or operation and the amount
of time and money you have for investment in your hobby.

Where space is limited, the smaller
gauges will of course have to be
used regardless of any other desires or conditions. But even
where space is unlimited it may be
wise to choose a small gauge if
that serves the particular inter-
ests of the builder. Since trolley
systems are more compact than
steam systems, it is often possible to use a larger scale where
otherwise a smaller one would have
to do. We pointed out that O gauge
trolley system would operate on a
9" radius track. Such a track is
only 20" in overall diameter for a
full circle where toy tracks in O
gauge are 32" in diameter and a
radius of 36" is considered a minimum for steam type railroad models. HO gauge (railroad) will operate on a 24" radius. So an O
gauge trolley system will not require as much room as an HO railroad system.

The smaller the gauge the more
difficult to build (if you are all
thumbs) and the less detail that
can be incorporated. On the other
hand, the smaller gauges require
less detail to make them appear
realistic because they are appar-
ently seen from a greater distance
where detail would not be visible.
Small gauges are less costly to
build but in making a large layout
require more of everything to fill
up a space of a given size. The
small size gauges are particularly
desirable if your preference lies
in laying out scenery rather than
operating.

From an operating standpoint it is
conceded that the larger gauges
perform better than the smaller
ones. For one thing there is a
greater choice of power drives and
motors as the scale size increases.
Certain items such as signals and
lighting systems are hard to reduce
to scale size. In general the larger size power units are more re-
liable and care free than the small
ones. From what has been said here
the neophite should be able to make
his choice based on the availabil-
ity of space, inherent interest
and financial budget.

In the overhead wire system of power distribution it is not necessary
to insulate the wheels of the trucks
from their axles as both running
rails serve as a common return for
the electric circuit. This is a much
simpler method than the now popular
"two-rail" system used in larger
steam type layouts. Either direct
current or alternating current can
be used for propulsion. This means
you can use the same type of power
equipment provided for toy or model
systems. In the development of our
theme we will describe the construction of a simple layout, then point
out ways how the system can be en-
larged to cover any type of trolley
operation. This method of explanation
will also serve as an introduction
to other more extensive systems.

The experience you gain in trolley
line modeling will always prove
useful in other railroad building.

So, why not be a model trolley line
operator. It's lots of fun. It will
give you no end of pleasant evenings
at home. If you have youngsters they
too will enjoy working and playing
with Dad and there is much to be
gained in this kind of companionship.
So - read on - let's get busy and
build that trolley line.

For plans of this car see page 65.

This is one of the types built by
the Cincinnati Car Co., and was a
very popular car in its day. You
will find plans for five different kinds of cars beginning at
page 62.

Chapter 2

PLANNING THE LAYOUT

Planning the layout is the first step. A toy railroader usually trys to lay as much track as he can in a given space without regard to an operating program; the experienced model railroader plans his track to provide the kind of operation he wants to have. Both must fit their plans to a prescribed space. It's like building a house. Before an architect plans a house he wants to know the size and shape of the lot, which way it faces, etc. Then he does his best to give his house the shape and appearance that will fit the lot and location.

Since we are going to build a trolley line we need only give thought to the considerations that apply to such a line. So let's assume we are the committee charged with making a survey and planning a transportation route. Here are the particular points to keep in mind:

1. What kind of a line are we going to build? Perhaps a city line following a prescribed route from one end of the city to another. Not particularly a straight route but one with a turn here and there . Or maybe one that connects two adjacent cities, extends from a city into the rural areas terminating in a smaller village. Again our project may call for an interurban line from 25 to 100 miles long linking a number of cities, villages, farm areas and manufacturing districts. You may have in mind an existing line you wish to model or you may be thinking of some places that should have transportation facilities. Or, there is nothing to stop you from dreaming up something based on hypothetical situations. Whatever your project, it should suggest scenery as well as a track plan.

2. What kind of service is the line to provide? This takes into account the scheduling of the runs, number of cars required and type of equipment. City lines have cars on frequent schedule using a two track system or providing passing tracks where meets are to be made. Interurban service is many times adequately provided for by a single car shuttling back and forth over the line. Such service could function with a single track without sidings. If the line is to carry freight, baggage and mail then more than one kind of car is called for.

Extra tracks at terminals may be needed for loading. A storage yard, a car shed, maintenance pit and other items are needed, when heavy service is planned. There is also the possibility of branch lines calling for interchange of passengers and freight. Think of some of the electric lines you have ridden on or know about and analyze their operations as a clue to the service you want to duplicate in your line.

3. Are there any obstacles to overcome? These may be real or fiction. Real obstacles are those you face in utilizing your own space. There may be pipes in the way to hamper your right-of-way, washtubs, furnaces, fruit closets and sometimes masonry walls. Fiction obstacles are those you wish to create. These may be grades, tunnels, embankments to cut thru, rivers to span, highways that must underpass the line or be protected with warning signals and gates. Very often you can use your real obstacles in creating fiction ones. Thus pipes may be hidden in a mountain with the tracks circling the mountain. A hole in the wall can be disguised as a tunnel opening. Running on two levels is often necessary to conserve space and reducing from two to one track is one way to squeeze a rail line thru a tight spot. All these "hazards", real or otherwise, should be fitted in to the layout and operational scheme.

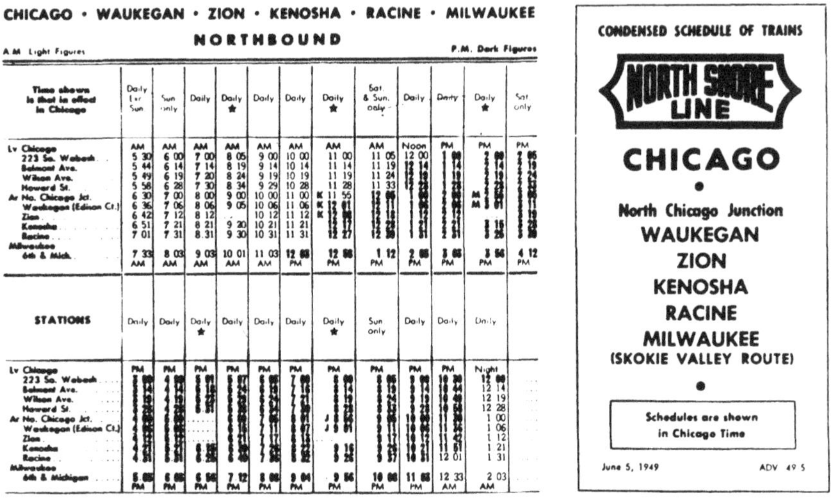

CHICAGO · WAUKEGAN · ZION · KENOSHA · RACINE · MILWAUKEE

NORTHBOUND

A.M. Light Figures   P.M. Dark Figures

CONDENSED SCHEDULE OF TRAINS

NORTH SHORE LINE

CHICAGO
•
North Chicago Junction
WAUKEGAN
ZION
KENOSHA
RACINE
MILWAUKEE
(SKOKIE VALLEY ROUTE)
•

Schedules are shown
in Chicago Time

June 5, 1949   ADV 49 S

FIG. 3 TYPICAL INTERURBAN TIMETABLE.

4. Don't overlook the timetable! Just running a car or two on a track without regard to timing is not planned operation. This does not mean that you must tie yourself down to a fixed operating procedure but it does imply an analysis of the proper use of track, sidings and terminals so that when you do run your trains they seem to be going somewhere, making meets and stops enroute and getting to a terminal after a definite number of "miles" of travel. This is particularly desirable when more than one car is running at the same time and there is the possibility of passing or overtaking another car. Thus local and express cars may use the same track but follow different timing. Freight and passenger cars may operate at different speeds and be subject to rules, or train orders.

5. Make a drawing of your space to scale. This is an important step in your planning. The drawing should show the location of every obstacle and give accurate dimensions of all space that can be utilized. Show on this drawing the area which will be used for the tables or shelves on which the track will be built. Have several black line prints made of this drawing and use the prints for making suggested track layouts. On the preliminary drawings only a single line need be drawn for the track. When your plans have jelled and you are ready to begin construc-

tion, draw the final plan on the original space drawing and again have several prints made. Each of these prints is then used for detailing some part of the work. Thus one print will serve for laying out the overhead system, another for the scenery details, another for signals and track accessories, etc.

This planning is definitely part of the fun in building a model system. It will whet your imagination and stimulate your observation as you search for new ideas and test your plans against actual prototype experience. You will be looking at the overhead wire construction to see how it is supported, to see where the trolley "frogs" are placed in the wire so the trolley always follows the car. You will get a new kick out of talking to a motorman or "pilot" to get pointers on operation and rules. With your camera you will visit the car barns to get pictures of the detail parts of cars so you can build your model to prototype exactness. And you will get a big thrill just watching every detail of trolley operation. It may all seem complicated to you now, but don't worry about that, because you will take one step at a time. The purpose of this Guide is to help you in your planning to suggest a plan of procedure and to avoid making mistakes.

8

In mentioning mistakes, perhaps the most discouraging one is "to bite off more than you can chew". Remember: Rome was not built in a day! So don't hurry. This hobby of building a trolley system is one to be enjoyed for a long time. Just because there are so many "angles" does not mean all have to be accomplished at once. You can start your project by laying a single section of straight track, acquiring or building a single car and with a minimum of electrical equipment start operations. Then add some more track, put in a passing siding, add another car or a trailer. That is the way many of the real trolley systems were built. Perhaps some member of your family will give you a lift in building scenery or you will find a friend who will be more than willing to share the hobby with you.

The next step is to develop a track layout, keeping in mind the various points mentioned in the preceding section. This layout should fulfill your idea of the kind of line you want, the service it should provide, the obstacles to be overcome and the timing or operational scheme. The best way to approach this, is to analyze a number of basic track layouts and how each provides an operational pattern. From there on it's just a matter of combining those which fit your space and project. When it comes to building you start with one basic part and add on others as time permits. But it is well to have the master plan in mind so that each part fits in to eventually make the whole.

Let's begin with the two forms that are easiest to build - the straight section shown in figure 4, and the loop shown in figure 5. The straight track is what is known as a "point-to-point" route from terminal A to B. It is one rather common in actual trolley line construction but restricted to one car shuttling back and forth. There are no turnouts or passing sidings so there can be no meets. This simple scheme may be varied by adding curved sections and winding in and out just as long as it remains a single track with two terminals. The loop is an endless chain without any terminal points. It offers an opportunity of running several cars, one behind the other, but it is difficult to maintain proper spacing with one operating circuit for all. Other forms of loops are shown in figures 6 (known as a "dumbell" or "dog-bone" pattern). The loop may take any overall form and remains a loop just as long as no crossings or turnouts are included. From an operational point of view, these track patterns are very restricted.

In diagram 7 is shown a passing siding. This is the first basic unit to be added to the simpler forms just described to provide an operating "angle". With two cars running on the same track, one will take the siding so the other can either overtake it, if traveling in the same direction or make a "meet" if traveling in the opposite direction. The passing siding can be combined with a station or left "in the woods" as desired. Here are a few things to keep in mind with passing sidings:

FIG. 4 STRAIGHT TRACK FOR POINT TO POINT OPERATION.

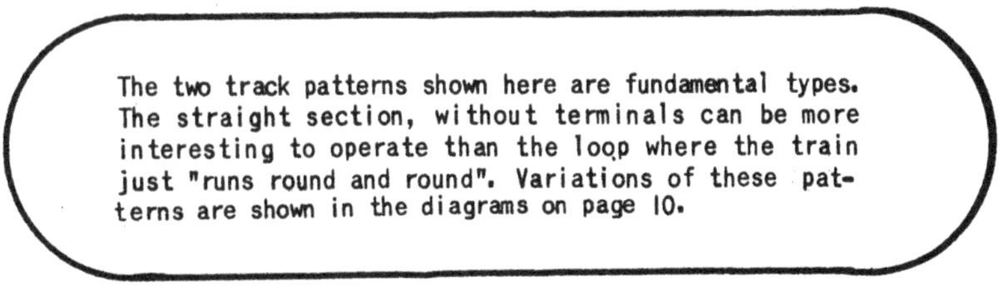

The two track patterns shown here are fundamental types. The straight section, without terminals can be more interesting to operate than the loop where the train just "runs round and round". Variations of these patterns are shown in the diagrams on page 10.

FIG. 5 LOOP TRACK LAYOUT FOR CONTINUOUS OPERATION.

FIG. 6 DOG-BONE OR DUMB-BELL LOOP PATTERN.

An endless chain. The layout is still a "loop" even though the
shape of the pattern differs. A layout such as this offers no
operating problems.

FIG. 7. STRAIGHT SECTION WITH PASSING SIDING.

The "point-to-point" scheme with a passing siding permits two
trains to run in opposite directions and "meet" at the siding.
Each train must reverse at each end to make its return trip.

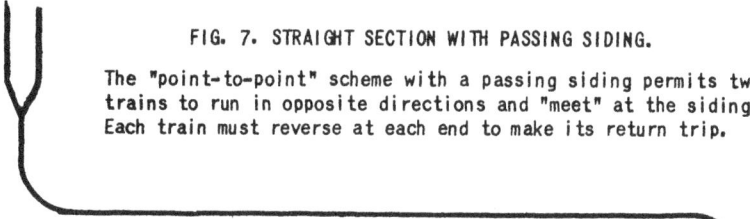

FIG. 8. STRAIGHT TRACK WITH WYE TYPE TERMINALS

Another "point-to-point" layout but providing a turnout at each
end which may be used as a terminal. As many as four different
trains can operate in sequence over this layout, with three laying over at the terminals.

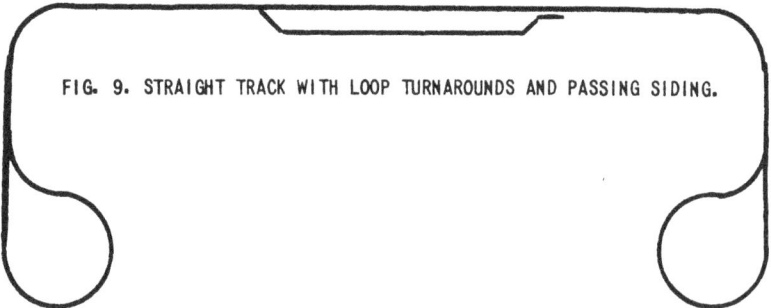

FIG. 9. STRAIGHT TRACK WITH LOOP TURNAROUNDS AND PASSING SIDING.

A combination of the "dog-bone" loop with a passing siding at
mid-point of the layout. Trains run in the same direction and do
not have to reverse at the terminals. While this is a simple
layout to build it offers real life railroading.

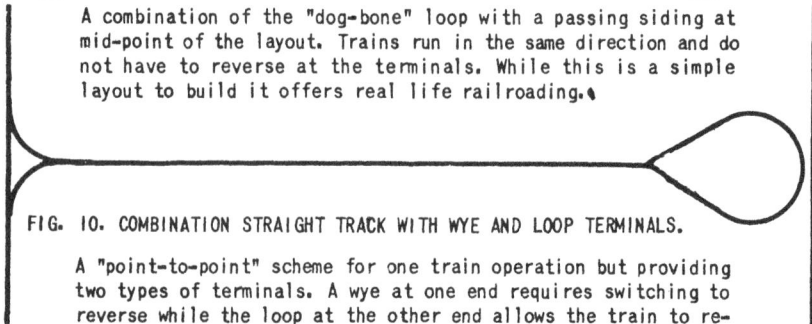

FIG. 10. COMBINATION STRAIGHT TRACK WITH WYE AND LOOP TERMINALS.

A "point-to-point" scheme for one train operation but providing
two types of terminals. A wye at one end requires switching to
reverse while the loop at the other end allows the train to return without reversing.

1. The siding track must be long enough to accomodate the longest train to be parked without "fouling" at the switches. The fouling point of a switch is that point on the trailing side of the frog, beyond which a car standing on the branch track will not be struck by one moving on the main track. Enough extra length must be included to permit a train to coast to a stop before overtaking the fouling point on the exit switch.

2. When the passing siding is used exclusively for meets the switches are "sprung" so the inferior train (or first scheduled to arrive) will automatically take the siding and the superior train the main line. Switches equipped with springs are normally held in the position governing their route but the points will move to the other position under pressure of the wheels, when cars trail over the switch. Thus one switch will be normal (straight) and the other reversed (set for the siding).

3. When the use of the passing siding may be optional, for either train, the switches are equipped with a switch motor (single or double solenoid) so they can be aligned to either position by an electric circuit operated from the control board. Or the switch points can be moved manually. For those who like automatic controls there are ways in which the switch machines are energized from track controlled circuits by the wheels of the cars as they pass over special sections of tracks known as "ramps".

4. Some provision is made to stop the car as soon as it has been placed properly on the passing siding. This is done by sectionalizing the running rails, between the switches so the car arrives on a dead section or one that can be controlled from an independent circuit. When it is time for the car to leave the siding (after the other train has passed the siding) this circuit is closed either from the control board or energized from the main line track by the train which is traveling on the main line.

The various constructional and operating details mentioned above will be described fully in other sections of this Guide. They are mentioned here to show the tie-up between track patterns and operational schemes. The passing siding may be added to any track layout but its position should be chosen with regard to timing as well as general space utilization. Never put a passing siding in a curved part of the track as this is an operational hazard.

A simple terminal arrangement is shown in diagram 8. This employs a "wye" switch so the tracks to the terminal will be symmetrical around the platforms. The switch may be hand or electric operated to permit a car to use either terminal track at the discretion of the operator. This terminal scheme permits the use of two or more cars to make runs over a single track by running in rotation. By using a terminal at each end, more cars may be added and run in sequence. With a passing siding at the mid-point of the run cars may move in both directions and pass each other enroute. On a long run several passing sidings are in order.

Diagram 9 shows a loop added to the end of a single track as a turn around. With this type of pattern a car always runs in the same direction without changing trolleys or reversing the motor. The "wye" scheme shown in diagram 10 is another way of turning a car or train around. A wye takes more room than a loop but on city systems is used for convenience. Practically every type of track layout will use these basic forms in one manner or another. In the diagrams that follow a number of suggested layouts are shown. Study these with reference to your own space and the operating scheme you plan to follow. From here on, you are on "your own" as the civil engineer in charge of track-work.

See page 68 for a complete list of articles published in leading magazines on subjects of interest to traction modelers.

11

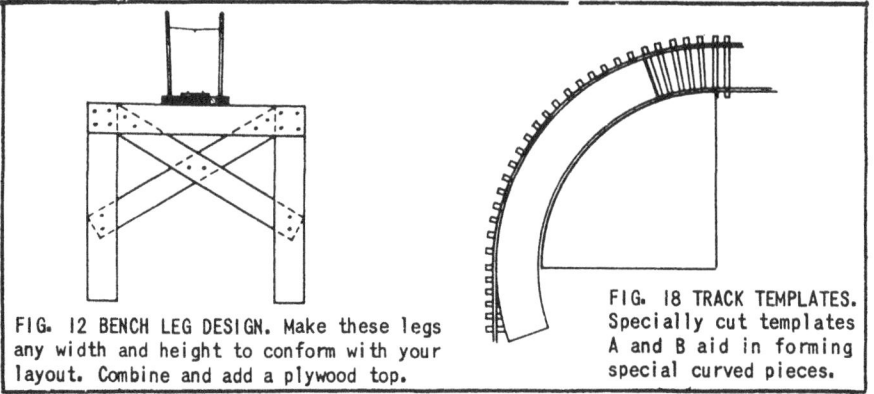

FIG. 12 BENCH LEG DESIGN. Make these legs any width and height to conform with your layout. Combine and add a plywood top.

FIG. 18 TRACK TEMPLATES. Specially cut templates A and B aid in forming special curved pieces.

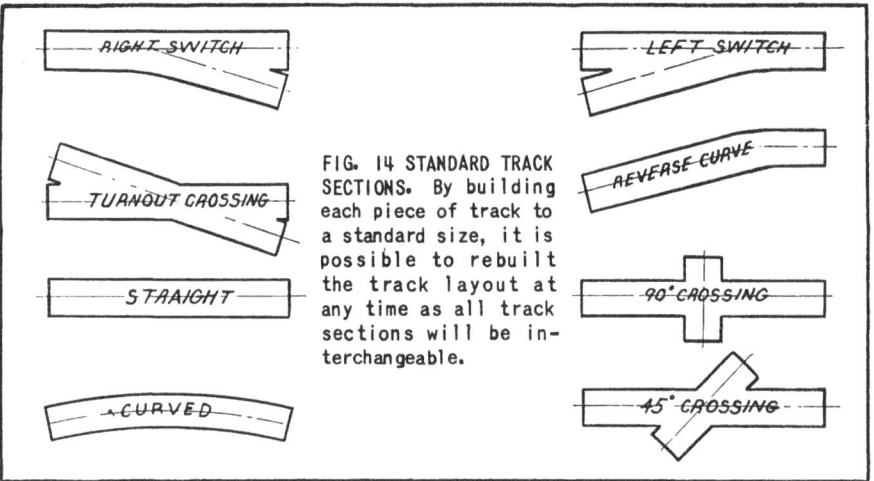

RIGHT SWITCH

LEFT SWITCH

TURNOUT CROSSING

REVERSE CURVE

STRAIGHT

90° CROSSING

CURVED

45° CROSSING

FIG. 14 STANDARD TRACK SECTIONS. By building each piece of track to a standard size, it is possible to rebuilt the track layout at any time as all track sections will be interchangeable.

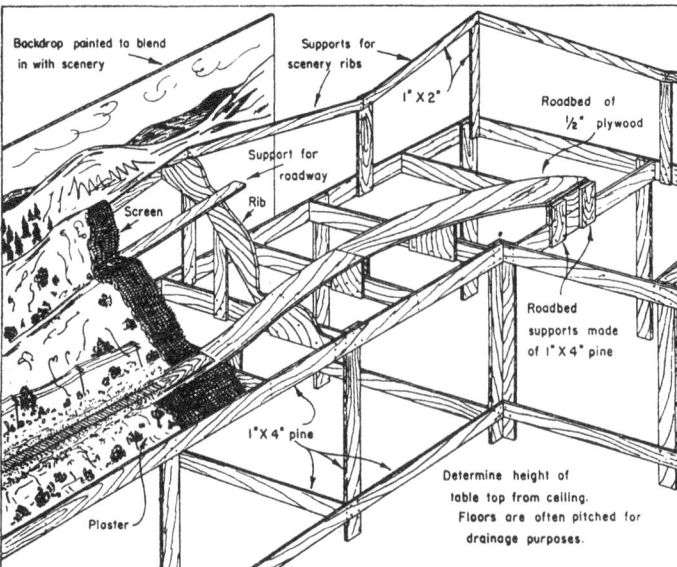

Backdrop painted to blend in with scenery

Supports for scenery ribs

1" X 2"

Roadbed of ½" plywood

Support for roadway

Rib

Screen

Roadbed supports made of 1" X 4" pine

1" X 4" pine

Plaster

Determine height of table top from ceiling. Floors are often pitched for drainage purposes.

FIG. 13 TABLE CONSTRUCTION. This is what is called an "open-top" or skeleton type table. From a base level, supports are added for the track and road ways. The in-between space is then molded into shape by applying plaster over fine screening.

Chapter 3

BENCH AND TRACKWORK

Let us assume that the preliminary survey has been completed, the route plotted, all franchises for right of way secured and the necessary bond issue floated. In other words you are now ready to begin building. Whether it's a "city" line which will extend its track to the country, or an "interurban" line that will connect several cities it is all the same to the crew that has to lay the track, string the trolleys and get everything in shape for the boys that will operate. In this chapter we will discuss the benchwork and the track building.

Benchwork. The very first question to answer is: on what are you going to build? If you must use an old table that is headed for the scrap pile, all right but in the end you will find an open top bench the most satisfactory foundation and a wise investment. The bench should be from 30" to 42" high using the lower dimension if you're going to have a mountain section or second level , and the upper dimension if your terrain is going to be more or less level. The width of the bench will be determined by the number of tracks, scenery and buildings to be included. It should be at least 18" wide for straightaway sections and up to 30" wide for loops and terminals. However, do not consider these dimensions maximum but let them take whatever values are dictated by your layout. Allow 4 to 6" for each track and another 6" to 12" for background and track accessories.

The bench legs are constructed as shown in figure 12. One such leg for each 2' of length will be ample. Tie the legs together with a horizontal board, 4" wide, run along the top edges (front and back). Anchor against the wall where ever possible. A narrow shelf, held up by brackets, can be used in place of the bench for stretches of single track between terminals. The top of the bench is left open purposely for reasons which will be explained lat-

er. A baseboard 6" wide is laid across the top of the benches in conformity to the track layout. This board will have to be cut and fitted to follow the straight and curved sections of track. To this board will be laid the track and trolley supports.

The top of the bench is left open rather than closing it in with a table top so that a rolling rather than a flat terraine can be built upon it, but if you feel that it will be easier for you to construct your track on a flat surface, then cover your benchtop with plywood panels - 3/16" or 1/4" thick, but add the base board over the panels as you will need a strong support for trolley poles. With an open top bench, the intervening space will be filled in with wire screening (1/4" mesh hardware cloth is excellent), and this will be shaped to represent valleys, embankments and the usual irregularity of the ground surface. Then later this screening will be covered with plaster to simulate the ground itself.

The baseboard mentioned above may be omitted from the bench top and made the basis of each section of track. This plan has the merit of later interchangeability if it is desired to add or shift track units to form a new routing. Whether you build your track in sections or on location is a matter of preference. We mention both methods and the advantages of each for your own guidance. The particular advantage of the on location method is that it is continuous and requires less time for cutting rails while the sectional method is time saving when a number of similar track sections can be constructed using jigs and templates.

It is beyond the scope of this Guide to attempt to detail every step in the construction program. Much ex - cellent material has already been written and should be consulted by those who need additional guidance or wish to review several methods of construction before determining on their own. A list of magazine articles and books bearing on the subject matter of each chapter will be found appended at the close of the Guide.

Trackwork Standards. The National Model Railroad Association (NMRA) has developed standards for all gauges which apply to track building and trolley wire construction. These standards are shown in table form on the inside cover. Consult and follow them at all times. By so doing your track will be properly constructed so any cars built to like standards will operate satisfactorily.

It is also a good plan to standardize your track sections as to length, radius and degree. Since rail is available in 3 ft. lengths, sections of track should be 3 ft. long or some equal part of 3 ft., as 12", 18" or 24". The radius of curvature will depend on whether you are building a city track or for country operation. The usual street curves are made to a 35' radius (9" in O gauge and 5" for H O gauge). Interurban cars should have as large a radius as your space allows but 100' should be a minimum (24" for O and 15" for H O gauge). The length of a curved section should be equivalent to 45° (1/8th circle). Switches and crossings should be built to the same dimensions so they can be interchanged with their track section count - erparts.

In laying out your track patterns you first locate the center line and then work out and in from that. For curved track use a compass consist - ing of a heavy cord with a nail at - tached to one end and a pencil to the other, adjusting the length of cord to fit the radius. If you do not have a 45° triangle for laying out the length of the curved section, lay out a right angle with a carpenters square and then bisect (halve) this angle by marking arcs with your compass and drawing the bisecting line as shown in figure 15.

Track Construction Methods. A section of track should consist of a roadbed board at least 3/4" thick and wide enough to include the trolley poles at each side of the track. For O gauge 6" is ample width and other gauges in proportion. Chamfer the two top edges so the roadbed will appear to taper to the sides. Shellac the boards on all sides to prevent warping. For ballast, the board can be covered with strips of slate roofing paper cut wide enough so it will lap over the edges of the board to simulate the road-bed grading. Some prefer to build up the ballast by cementing loose gravel in between the ties and over the roadbed board. This looks nice but is not too practical because the gravel works loose. There are available several types of ready made road bed board some of which include the ties. The use of any of these track parts is optional with the builder.

The next step is to lay the ties to the roadbed board (over the roofing paper ballast). Wood ties may be used or a clothboard tie strip. Ties are more realistic but troublesome to lay, the tie strip material is easy to handle and because it is thin will appear to show only a small section of the tie above the ballast. For curved sections the webb between the ties of the cloth

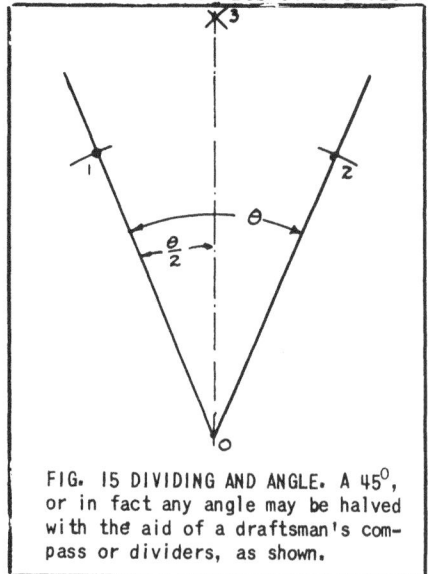

FIG. 15 DIVIDING AND ANGLE. A 45°, or in fact any angle may be halved with the aid of a draftsman's compass or dividers, as shown.

board strip are cut away on one side to permit shaping the tie strip to the curve. Wood ties are held with small wire nails driven thru the approximate center of the tie. Use a straight edge or an improvised tie gauging template to keep the ties in line and properly separated. The space between ties should be slightly wider than the width of a tie. With tie strip it is necessary to nail it down on every tenth tie.

The rail comes next. Locate one of the rails on the ties and spike it down, first on every third or fourth tie for a convenient stretch then sight along this rail and straighten out any kinks as you add the in between spikes. Lay the parallel rail using a track gauge to maintain proper "gauge" spacing. The track gauge is so built that it automatically expands the gauge distance on curved tracks. Do not spike the rail to the

first and last ties because it will be necessary to slip the "fishplate" connectors onto the rail ends when joining the sections later. To have a well constructed track, the rail should be spiked on both sides at each tie. This means a total of four spikes for each tie. This calls for a lot of work but it is labor well spent.

Laying Track in City Streets. For city tracks the rail is laid either on ties or directly onto the base board. For curves a template cut from masonite just wide enough to fit between the rails, makes an excellent guide. (SEE figure 18). The method of laying rail and gauging is the same as just described under the previous heading. After the rail is in place the street is completed by filling in and around the track to simulate the usual paving.

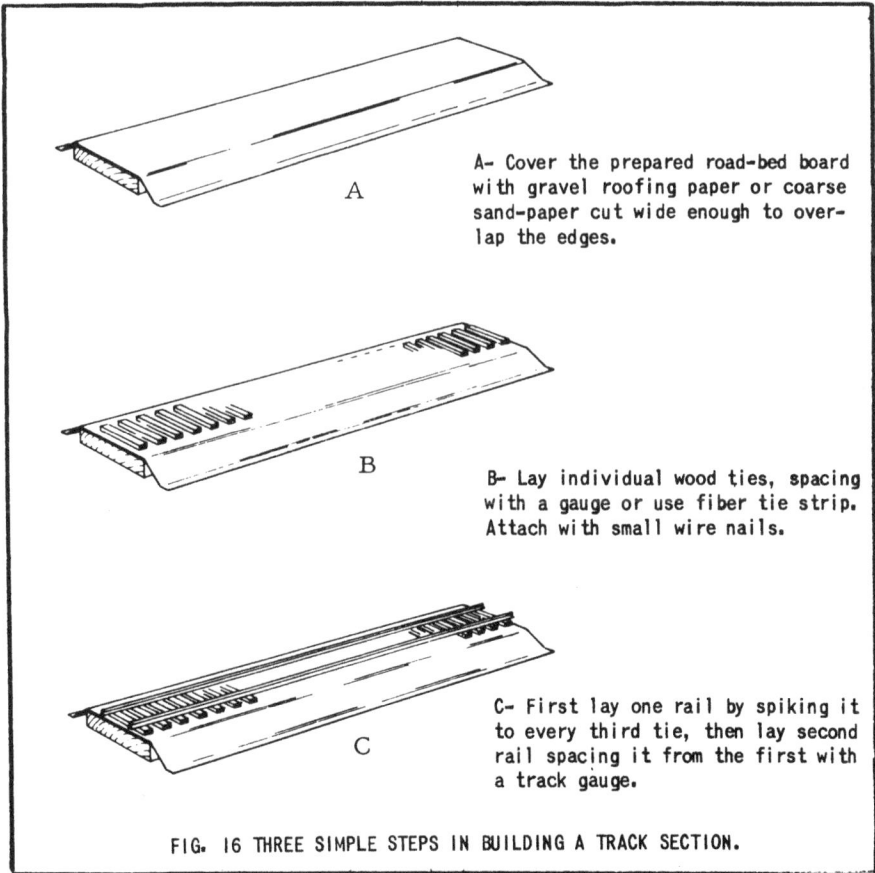

A- Cover the prepared road-bed board with gravel roofing paper or coarse sand-paper cut wide enough to overlap the edges.

B- Lay individual wood ties, spacing with a gauge or use fiber tie strip. Attach with small wire nails.

C- First lay one rail by spiking it to every third tie, then lay second rail spacing it from the first with a track gauge.

FIG. 16 THREE SIMPLE STEPS IN BUILDING A TRACK SECTION.

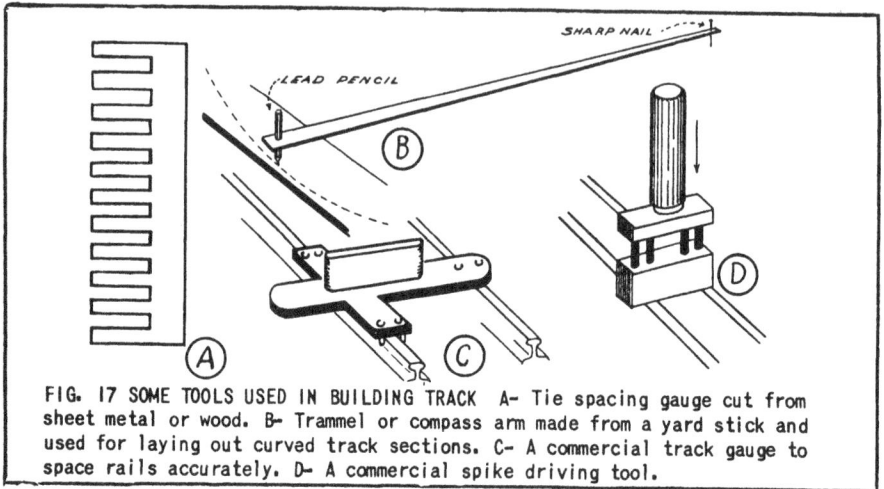

FIG. 17 SOME TOOLS USED IN BUILDING TRACK A- Tie spacing gauge cut from sheet metal or wood. B- Trammel or compass arm made from a yard stick and used for laying out curved track sections. C- A commercial track gauge to space rails accurately. D- A commercial spike driving tool.

To "pave" the street proceed as follows: First shellac the roadbed board (if this was not done previously) then make a mix of patching plaster and spread this in between the rails and the street curbing line to the level of the rail head.

Let this set to the point where it no longer flows freely then scrape out a groove along the inside edges of the track for the wheel flanges to run in. This scraping can be done very nicely if you prepare a stick or metal tool of the proper size and just pull it along the rail. Wet the tool from time to time so it does not tear into the plaster.

You can use plaster of paris in place of patching plaster if you want a smooth finish like a concrete street. But since plaster of paris sets rapidly you should use it in small mixes or add a little marshmallow root to slow up the setting. A little experimenting will tell you just how much of this you need. There are many kinds of prepared modelling plasters on the market but all should be sampled before attempting to pave a complete street.

The space between rails (inside the track) can be covered with brick paper to represent paving blocks or brick and the balance of the street painted. Curbing can be added by using thin strips of wood or a side walk effected by laying strips of board at each side of the street. This board can be painted to represent the walk and grass simulated with "flock" (Texcote) or painted on with green colors. These details belong to the scenery division.

Building Turnouts (switches). A switch is needed where ever the track divides into two. In railroad language switches are called "turnouts" because one track turns out of the other. It is better to use the term "turnout" for these track diverting devices because the word switch is commonly used to indicate an electrical device for controlling a circuit. The important parts of a turnout are: the movable points, frog, guard rails and point shifting device or "motor".

The points include the moving and fixed pieces which extend from the beginning or point of the switch to the frog. The movable rails are bent and tapered to fit snug against the "stock" rails. The frog forms the intersection between the running rails at their point of crossing. Switch frogs are numbered in accordance with their degree of tangency or "slope". A number 4 frog is one that slopes or spreads out one inch in four inches of run. The radius of curvature of the turnout is that of the curved section of the diverting track. The guard rails are placed alongside the main rails opposite the frog to guide the wheels into the proper channels at the frog and prevent them from climbing over the frog.

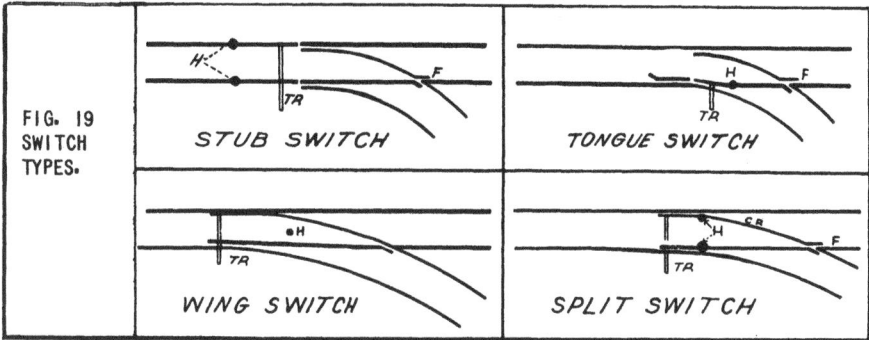

FIG. 19 SWITCH TYPES.

STUB SWITCH

TONGUE SWITCH

WING SWITCH

SPLIT SWITCH

The device for shifting the points into alignment for either route may be a simple lever for hand operation, a spring which biases the points to one position but permits movement to the other by the car wheels as they trail over the points, or an electrically operated switch motor. Of these there are several good types consisting either of a single or double set of coils. The single coil type must be energized as long as it is to hold the switch in its operated position for when the coil is not in use the points return to their normal position by spring tension. The double coil type is operated to either position by momentarily energizing the proper coil from a push button or lever key at the control point.

Diagram 19 shows four styles of switches. The tongue type, which has a single movable point is still used by trolley lines in city streets and the trolley builder modeling city lines should use this type whenever a switch is called for in a model city street. Other diagrams show various types of switch parts. Cast frogs at one time were very popular with model railroaders but many now prefer to build the frog from rail. This requires precise workmanship but the finished turnout is so much more realistic that the extra effort is well repaid.

The actual construction of a turnout is perhaps the most difficult part of any track laying project. If you have never tried your hand at this work before we suggest that you make a full size drawing of the turnout you intend to build. To make this drawing first lay out a section of straight track then superimpose a section of curved track with the straight and curved sections merging at the beginning end (called leading end) of the turnout. Where the curved and straight sections cross you have the frog. The rails between the frog and the beginning end of the switch are each made in two pieces, one which forms a "point" and the other called the "closure" rail.

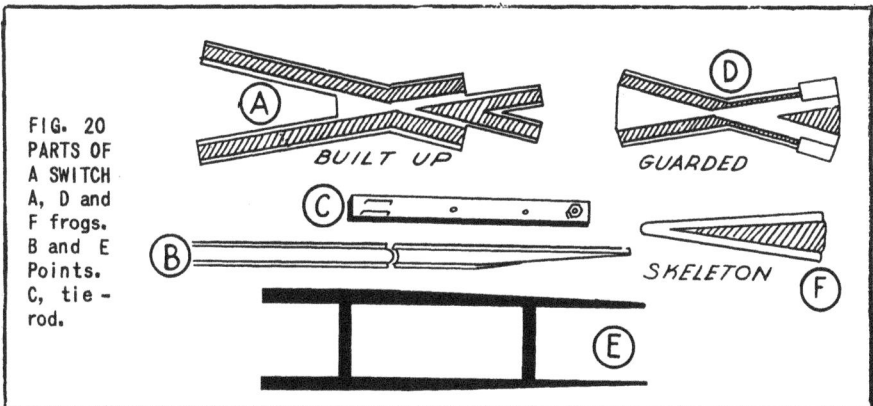

FIG. 20 PARTS OF A SWITCH A, D and F frogs. B and E Points. C, tie-rod.

BUILT UP

GUARDED

SKELETON

This last section is flared out at the frog somewhat in the shape of a "y" to form the passageway for the wheels and the "wing" of the frog. The two point rails are connected by two thin pieces of brass strip to make the movable point section. Note that when the points are in one position with one of the points snug against the stock rail, the other point is separated from its stock rail by a distance large enough to permit the car wheels to pass thru. If you have trouble in designing your switch, look at some pictures, or at an actual switch along the car or railroad tracks.

If you are going to build several turnouts to this design have blueprints made from your drawing and use these prints as templates in building the actual turnout. By this we infer that you build the turnout right on top of the drawing using the drawing to locate all the parts. When the turnout is complete tear the drawing away from the ties or use a razor blade and cut around each tie.

For the trolley builders who do not care to build their own tracks and turnouts we suggest the use of built up track sections. Turnouts to match this built up track are also available. There are also some concerns who will build your track to your own specifications. Such specially constructed track sections are well worth their cost. When requesting prices of a custom track builder give him all the details as to the kind of construction you desire and send him a simple sketch of your layout showing the important dimensions, location of turnouts, terminals, yards, etc. Be sure to mention the radius for all curved sections and the type of roadbed and ballast you desire him to supply.

For you who intend to build your own track we suggest a reading of some of the articles or a book devoted to track building. You will find a listing of these in the appendix.

Third Rail Construction. If you are modeling the type of interurban system using a third rail for power

pick-up then of course this will have to be included in your track work. Third rail dimensions have been standardized by the NMRA and these standards should be followed. Here are a few brief notes about third rail construction methods. It is standard practice to place the third rail on the outside of curved sections. At turnouts, the third rail is placed along the inside of the curved section and adjacent to the unbroken running rail. In this way there will be a continuous third-rail for either track from the turnout.

For O gauge systems a 1/16" square brass rod is used for the third rail. For the smaller gauges 3/64" square stock is used. Some prefer to use HO rail for O gauge third rail. Supports for the third rail are available in many forms: clips, special type screws with recessed heads, insulators made from beads with nails or screws to hold them in place. The third rail is either crimped in place or soldered to the tops of the screws or nails. Third rail supports are placed approximately every third or fourth tie, which ties should be longer than the others. The third rail should be slightly higher than the running rail so the collector shoes will not foul on the running rail when passing over crossings or switches.

These dimensions are all given in the standard sheets of the NMRA.

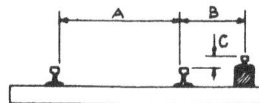

FIG. 21 THIRD RAIL DIMENSIONS. For O gauge the third rail top should be 1/8" above the top of the running rail. The distance from the gauge line of the track to the center of the third rail should be 11/16". No dimensions have been established for the other gauges as third rail is seldom used with them.

Chapter 4

THE OVERHEAD WIRE

It is the Overhead wire that sets off and makes trolleys more fascinating than other forms of model railroading. It is also the part that beginners shy away from because they feel it is too difficult to put up poles, string wires and keep the trolley on the track. But then any kind of work looks hard when viewed for the first time. If you follow the instructions given here and take each step in turn you will soon be an enthusiastic trolley modeler inviting your friends to join you in this fascinating branch of model railroading.

The overhead construction should not be undertaken until the trackwork is complete and been approved by the "brass hat" of the road. However, it is not recommended that a complete layout of track be completed before putting some of it to use as a trolley system. In a previous chapter it was suggested that a simple track system consisting of a single stretch of track with a single pass-

ing siding be built as the first unit. So, when this part of the trackwork has been completed lets proceed with the overhead construction as outlined in this section.

Check the completed track work by running a test car over it. It is assumed that you have a power car available for this purpose but since there is no trolley wire to power it, attach a suitable flexible wire to the trolley pole and use this as a feeder for the car in place of the trolley. The power supply is temporarily attached to the tracks and this flexible jumper wire. Operate the car slowly over the track and watch for any spots in the track that bind, spread or de-rail the wheels. If you find any troublesome parts it will be easier to correct them before the poles and overhead wires are in the way. Keep the test car handy as you will want to check the overhead construction as the work is in progress.

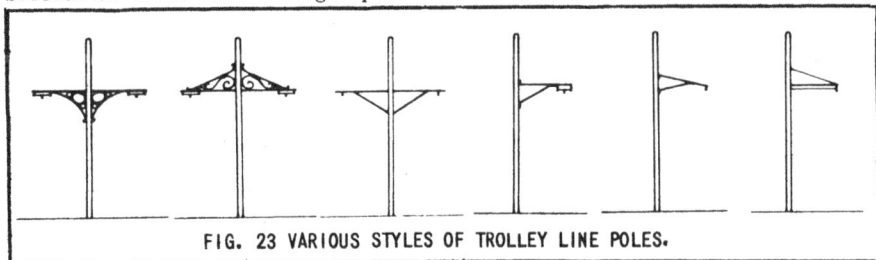

FIG. 23 VARIOUS STYLES OF TROLLEY LINE POLES.

FIG. 22 A VIEW ON THE MASON VIXEN LINES. An O gauge traction line built by R. K. Mason of Holland Mich. Photo by Art Sas.

Single Suspension System. There are three general types of construction that may be followed in the building of an overhead wire and any or all may be included in any layout. The types are:

1. Single suspension between two or more line poles (see note)
2. Bracket arm suspension.
3. Catenary

The catenary type of construction is the most difficult one in the smaller gauges while the single suspension is the simplest to build. The bracket arm, under certain conditions offers more rigidity than the single suspension type. Since most lines use either the single or bracket suspension methods these will be described first with a later section on the catenary system.

The line poles may be of wood or metal. Wood dowel rods of proper diameter (see table of dimensions) are less expensive than cold rolled steel rods but the metal rods have the advantage of serving as a conductor to the line wires. With wood poles it is necessary to run a wire up an occasional pole to feed the trolley wire. Metal poles are more rigid and if wood poles are used it may be desirable to guy these.

In the chapter on trackwork it was suggested that a 3/4" thick and 6" wide base board for the roadbed be used. The reason for these dimensions will now be apparent since space must be alloted for mounting

poles and the base board must be thick enough to make a rigid anchor for them. Poles are usually spaced 8-1/2 scale feet from each side of the track center line or 17 feet from pole to pole across the track. In O gauge this amounts to 4-1/4" leaving a distance of 7/8" between pole and the edge of the board, enough for tapering off the ballast effect. After the location of the poles has been established and marked off, holes are drilled (a snug fit for pole) and the poles anchored in these "post holes". Some prepared metal poles come provided with a threaded end so they can be secured with lock nuts, one above and one below the road bed board.

Poles are placed opposite each other but the spacing from pole set to pole set, and their actual location along the roadbed will depend on the trackwork. A good rule to follow is to see that a 65' long, 9' wide car will clear the poles. The recommended pole spacing is shown in table 24 along with wire sizes. The 8-1/2 ft. distance from the center of the track allows sufficient clearance but it is always well to check with your own equipment.

So, with the above general considerations in mind let's proceed with the hanging of the contact wire. Hang the tangent sections first, if possible. At first we will lay the contact wire in approximate position doing the final locating later when the "pull-offs" are added. In connection with this work it will be

FIG. 24 - TABLE OF POLE SPACING AND WIRE SIZES			
	O GAUGE	S GAUGE	HO GAUGE
POLE DIAMETER	1/4" WOOD OR METAL	3/16" METAL	1/8" METAL
SPACING CENTERS* ON TANGENTS ON CURVES	12" TO 16" 9" TO 12"	9" TO 14" 6" TO 10"	6" TO 12" 4" TO 9"
CONTACT WIRE SIZE**	24 GA	26 TO 30 GA	26 TO 30 GA
PULL OFF WIRE AND SUSPENSION	24 TO 26 GA	26 TO 30 GA	26 TO 30 GA
HEIGHT ABOVE RAIL	4-3/4 TO 5½'	3-9/16" TO 4-1/8"	2½" TO 3"
* WITH MANY GUYS AND PULL OFFS, CENTERS MAY BE INCREASED ** SPRING BRASS OR PHOSPHEROUS BRONZE. COPPER IS NOT RELIABLE.			

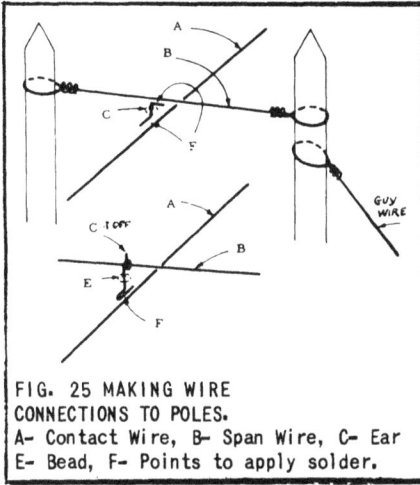

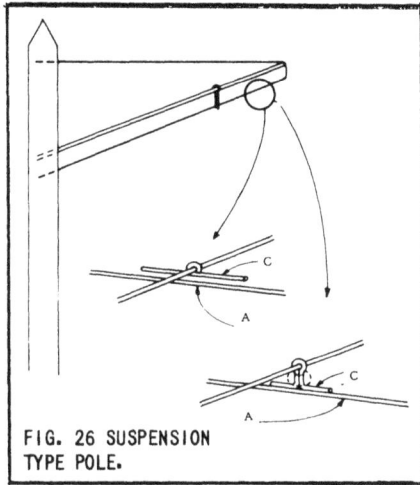

FIG. 25 MAKING WIRE
CONNECTIONS TO POLES.
A- Contact Wire, B- Span Wire, C- Ear
E- Bead, F- Points to apply solder.

FIG. 26 SUSPENSION
TYPE POLE.

FIG. 34 A VIEW ON R. M. WAGNER'S TROLLEY LAYOUT. Showing overhead wire construction

necessary to do some soldering and if this is an operation that you like to shun, read the paragraphs on soldering at the close of this section for suggestions on this subject. Actually soldering is not at all difficult if a few simple rules are followed and it is surprising how quickly one becomes expert.

The contact wire is not connected directly to the span wire but an intermediate wire known as an "ear" is used. These "ears" are best made from soft drawn wire (copper) and can take any of several shapes. The simplest scheme is to wrap the ear wire around the span wire as shown in figure 25, or form it like an open cotter pin. In the types shown

in figures 25 and 26 a small bead (from bead work supply house) is used as a spacer and to simulate an insulator. The style shown in figure 24 is made by bending the wire back on itself, then at the half way point bending at right angles. In the "Z" type one leg of the Z extends along the contact wire and the other leg is bent crosswise to follow the span wire.

Always solder the ear to the top of the overhead wire first, then to the contact wire. In figure 25 after prebending (use wire approximately 6" long at start), solder to top of contact wire, thread on the bead then wrap around span wire and solder. Cut off excess wire with wire

21

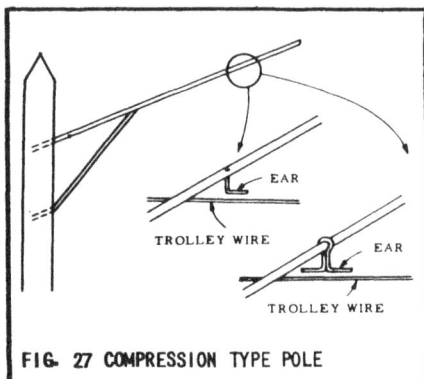

FIG. 27 COMPRESSION TYPE POLE

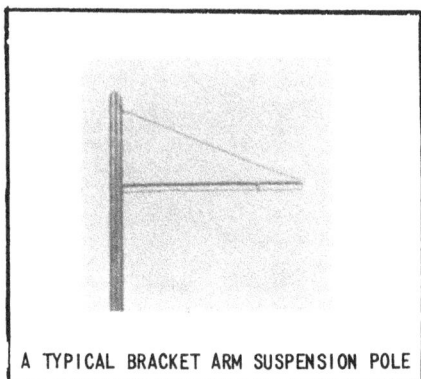

A TYPICAL BRACKET ARM SUSPENSION POLE

cutting pliers and start making the next ear. Continue this way from tangent to curve but leave some slack in contact wire along the curved sections. This slack will be taken up later when the pull-offs are attached. These are added last to add tension to the wire and to improve the appearance of the overhead work (more like the real thing).

Bracket Arm Suspension. This type probably will give a more rugged overhead but will require more accurate workmanship. The bracket arm suspension is most applicable to single and double track work while the single suspension span method works better where there are multiple tracks or over a complicated yard and switch layout. The spacing and location of poles is handled in the same way as for the simple suspension scheme. Generally a bracket line pole has a solid cross arm that fastens directly to the pole. In model work this is handled by drilling a hole in the pole to take the cross arm diameter.

With the poles in place attach a span wire between each set. For span wire you can use a size equal or slightly smaller than the contact wire. The span wire is wrapped around the pole and then twisted upon itself as shown in figure 25, in a neat manner. The other end of the wire is fastened in the same manner to the other pole of the set. It is not necessary to place this wire under tension but just have it straight and snug. Do not make the loops around the posts too

tight, at the start, as you may wish to move the wire up and down to properly locate the contact wire after it is attached to the spans. Later on, when the suspension is complete give these loops an extra twist with a pair of pliers to give them their final set. Put all spans in place before hanging the contact wire.

The simplest overhead construction is on a tangent track (straight portion). If a simple loop is to be your beginning, consider this as a series of tangents. From this point of view the most difficult wire arrangement can be hung. On tangents, for trolley car pole use, center the wire over the center line of the track. On curves the wire must be hung to the inside of the center line of the track for in this location the pole wheel or shoe remains parallel to the wire. This is true because the car overhangs the track when going around curves and the overhang of the middle of the car is always to the inside of the curve. This procedure will save excessive shoe wear and also prevent dewirements. In pantagraph operation the wire is staggered from pole support to pole support so that no one area on the pantagraph slide will be worn excessively.

If the track layout is to be sectionalized into blocks so different sections can be controlled independently it is much simpler to break up the track rather than the overhead wire. Overhead wire can be sectionalized if necessary but overhead insulation to have strength must be considerable oversize. On multiple tracks these overhead insulators become very noticeable. Not only that, the feeder wires from the control panel to each overhead unit are very much oversize too and the running of these in and around the poles detracts from the overall appearance. While finer wires can be used for feeders in order to make them less conspicuous such small wires have too high a resistance to carry the necessary current without excessive voltage drops. Consequently, if the overhead system can be considered as a single electrical network, its appearance can be kept much more to scale.

The suspension type of pole is shown in figure 26 and the type known as compression in **figure** 27. There are also combinations of these two types. The "ear" is made from copper wire (about the same size as the contact wire), like a simple wrap around or the more complicated "eyed" type. Tack solder one side first. Finish solder the other side, then finish solder the side tacked on. In figure 27 an "L" shaped ear which is easy to make is shown.

On a tangent the bracket poles may be placed on either side of the track. Here convenience is the rule. On curves it is best to have poles on the outside of the curve because it is a simple matter to install pull-offs, if on this side. True, the poles may be on the inside of a curve but, in this case, the cross arm length must be increased and the overhead construction is not as rigid.

Overhead Frogs. These are best made of sheet metal in the form of a "pan" as illustrated in figure 28. This type can be used with either pantagraphs or poles. The frogs are placed so they direct the trolley pole to follow the car direction.

One method of determining the proper location, above a turnout. One method of determining such a point is to take the sum of the lengths of the point and closure rails and divide by two. Locate these two points (one for each rail) as shown in figure 29. Then draw straight lines to the opposite points. Where the two lines intersect is where the overhead frog should be located. This is not a hard and fast rule. A trial run of the test car will verify the accuracy of the placement.

Fasten the frog to the trolley wire by bending a hook (about 105^0) in the contact wire and threading the hook end thru the prepared hole in the frog. While it is not necessary to solder the wire to the frog to do so will help keep the frog in alignment. A "Wye" type of frog will work for either right or left hand turnouts.

Overhead Crossing Frogs. These may be made up in the pan style, from sheet brass or copper. As far as the overhead is concerned the tracks can cross at any angle. The frog is always located at the point where the center lines of the tracks cross. When on a curve, where the overhead wires would normally cross.

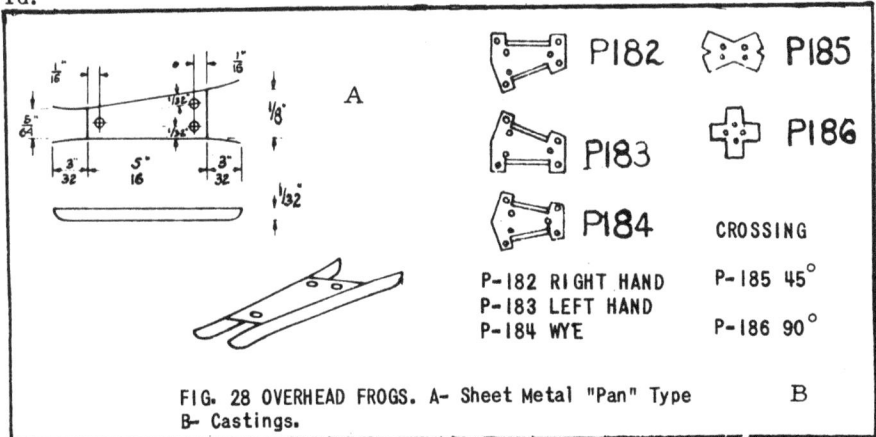

FIG. 28 OVERHEAD FROGS. A- Sheet Metal "Pan" Type B- Castings.

P182
P185
P183
P186
P184
CROSSING

P-182 RIGHT HAND
P-183 LEFT HAND
P-184 WYE

P-185 45°
P-186 90°

A

B

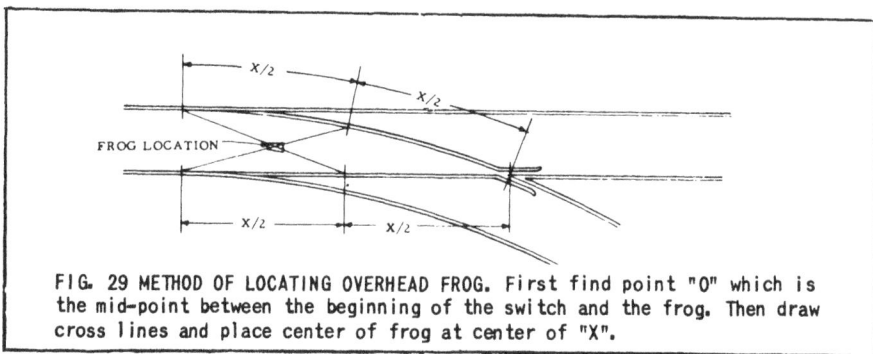

FIG. 29 METHOD OF LOCATING OVERHEAD FROG. First find point "O" which is the mid-point between the beginning of the switch and the frog. Then draw cross lines and place center of frog at center of "X".

Feeding and Splicing Wires. Feeders to the overhead should be as often as necessary to give the power cars uniform speed. For systems drawing much current feeders should be to every fourth pole (or even every second pole), but for systems requiring a minimum amount of current, a feeder to every tenth pole will be enough. Where metal poles are used the feeder may be connected directly to the lower end of the pole where it protrudes below the road bed board, or if it does not protrude then along the base where it will not be conspicuous.

In the case of wood poles the feeders must be run up the side of the pole and attached to the span wire. Another way to handle feeders is to carry them on telegraph poles alongside the track and run jumper wires from the feeders to the span wires. This can be made to look realistic if a little box to represent a tran-

sformer or oil switch is modeled and placed on the pole where the connection is made.

Where wires must be spliced, use a splicer member made from sheet metal, either flat stock or pan shaped. Both work equally well. In the former case be sure that the holes are drilled so the wires will be as close together as possible. If the wires lie one above the other, a lap solder joint can be made. The end of the lower wire should be tapered so it engages the trolley without a jerk. Another way is to use a short section of wire as a splice between the two contact wires. These methods are illustrated in figure *30*.

Another tip in hanging the contact wire is to use a "T" shaped jig and wire height gage that will automatically give the proper height at which to hang the spans and contact wire. This also serves as a rest for

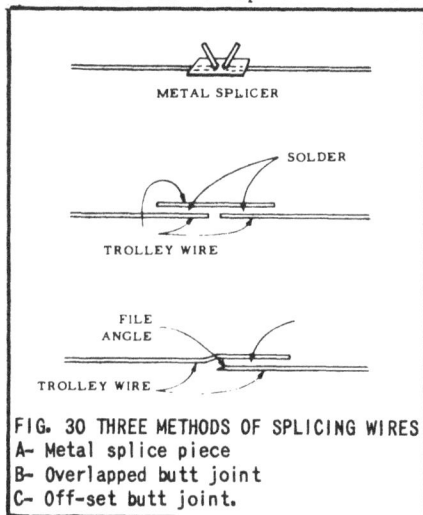

FIG. 30 THREE METHODS OF SPLICING WIRES
A- Metal splice piece
B- Overlapped butt joint
C- Off-set butt joint.

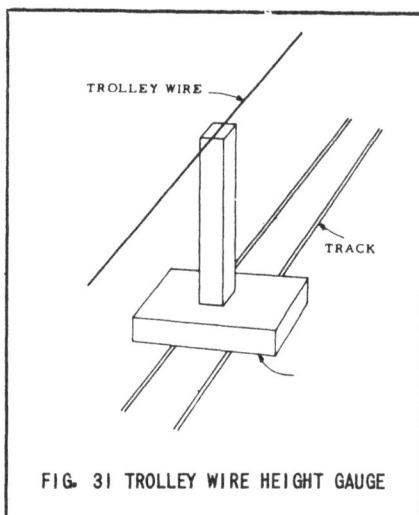

FIG. 31 TROLLEY WIRE HEIGHT GAUGE

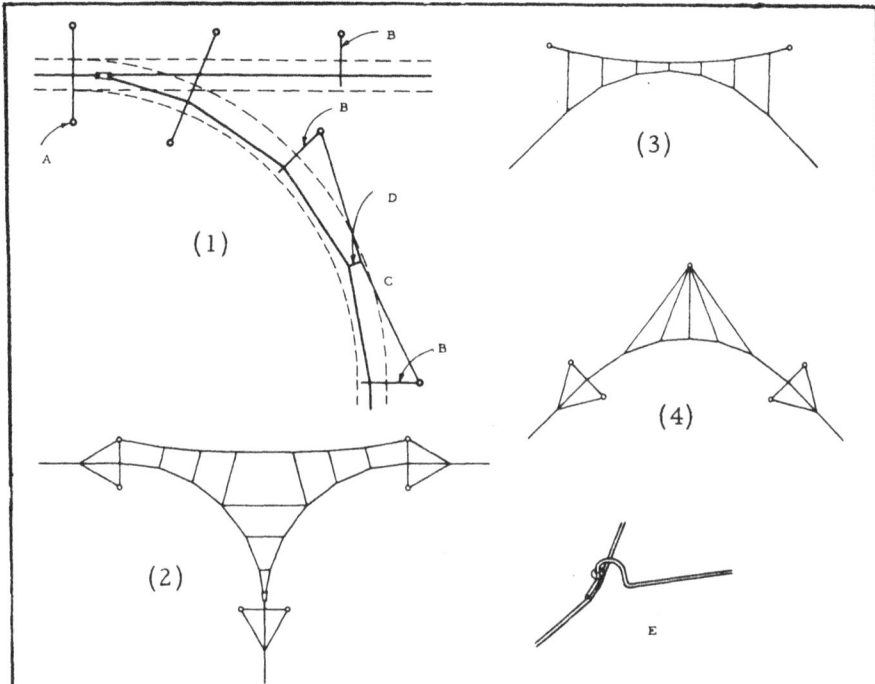

FIG. 32 VARIOUS WAYS TO ADD "PULL OFF" WIRES. A- Pole, B- Bracket arm, C- Back-bone Wire, D- Pull-off wire, E- Ear for attaching pull-off wire to contact wire. F- Contact wire.

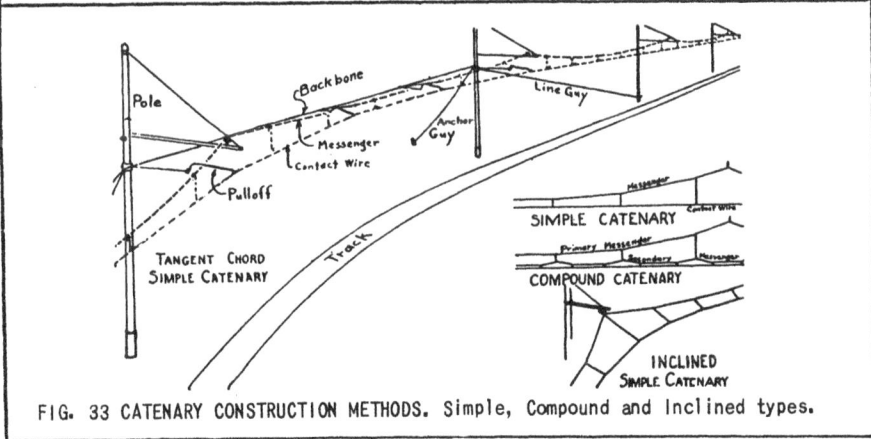

FIG. 33 CATENARY CONSTRUCTION METHODS. Simple, Compound and Inclined types.

the contact wire while soldering on the ears. Figure 31 illustrates this item.

Adding the Pull Off Wires. As the name implies, a "pull-off" wire is used to pull the wire into its proper location between poles and at the same time place the wire under tension. Diagram 32 shows the general idea followed in laying out the pull-offs. There is no particular rule to follow but try to keep the wires in some symmetrical arrangement so they look nice. The wire running from poles to pole to which the pull-offs are connected is known as the "backbone". The pull-off wire is never attached to the contact wire without the use of an ear just as the span and contact wires are attached.

Catenary System. The word "catenary" is a mathematical term to define the curve taken by a cord or wire allowed to hang free between two points of support. The amount of sag at the midpoint is dependent on the weight of the wire and the length of the span. In the simple form of catenary, there are two wires: the supporting wire which takes the shape of the catenary curve is called the "messenger" wire, the other, which is supported from this and which is in contact with the trolley wheel or pantagraph shoe is called the "contact" wire. This is better explained by the left-half part of diagram 33. (See page 25)

Another type, in which the contact wire is supported from an intermediate wire which in turn is supported from the messenger wire is called a compound catenary. The method of construction and the names of the parts are shown in diagram 33B.

There are two types of construction followed in putting up catenary overheads. One of these is known as the "inclined" catenary. In this scheme the contact wire is aligned on curves with inclined hangers. The position of these hangers will be dependent upon the relative weights of the contact wire and hangers and on the pull toward the center of the curve resulting from the tension in the wire as it goes around the curve. This type of construction is difficult to build and even though

it is the most common type used in prototype practice, we recommend that the simpler "tangent cord" method of construction be used.

In the tangent cord catenary construction method, the contact wire alignment is governed entirely by the pull-off wires as the hangers serve only to support the weight of the wire since the messenger wire is so arranged as to be directly above the contact wire at all points. Between pull-offs on sharp curves, and between points of support on wide curves, a section of tangent cord catenary will look exactly like a section of a similar length cut from a tangent.

Where pull-offs are required between points of support, they are attached to a supporting wire called a "backbone", strung between the nearest poles and outside of the curve, at the contact wire height (22 feet). This backbone wire is not needed if there is a pole for attaching each pull-off. On the other hand, where the backbone wire is used, additional poles may be needed at sharp curves to properly locate the backbone.

Pull-offs are also needed for the primary messenger wire, and these should be placed in a vertical line with the contact wire pull-off. In the case of the intermediate or secondary messenger wire, the pull-off is located above each bend in the

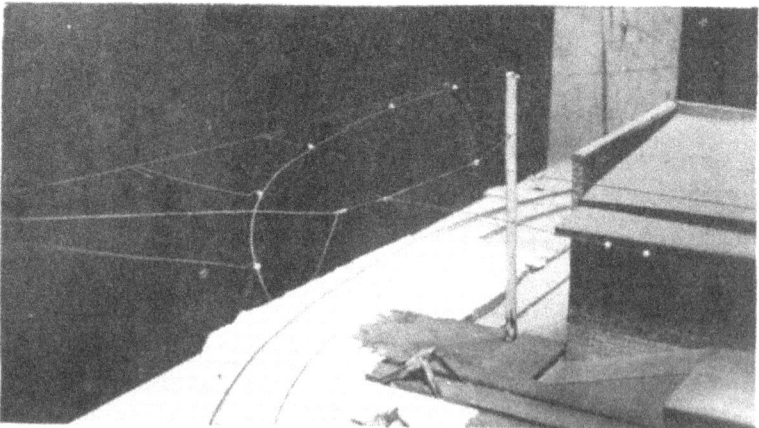

A VIEW ON R. M. WAGNER'S LAYOUT. Showing "pull-offs" on overhead construction.

FIG. 36 A VIEW ON THE TROLLEY LAYOUT OF THE NEW HAVEN SOCIETY OF MODEL ENGINEERS. Overhead wire system is well built and smooth operating.

contact wire. The length of the hanger wire used to support the contact wire from the messenger can be calculated for any span and sag but the best way to make up these parts is to first prepare a pattern for a standard span length, and then determine the size of each part from this pattern. Then make up jigs for assembling the sections.

Soldering Technique. Much of the success of the overhead work will depend on how you do your soldering. Now this may sound most complicated but it really isn't if you will follow a few simple rules. A little practice and you will soon consider yourself a master at the art. The operating results will repay any extra effort you put on developing a satisfactory soldering technique. A prime requisite is a clean iron that is not kept too hot. An example would be a 100 watt iron with small tip and with a 200 watt incandescent lamp in series with it. The beauty of this arrangement is that the iron is hot enough for small soldering work but not so hot that all the tinning on the tip keeps burning off.

A tip can be prepared by filing off all dirt from the copper tip in such a way that four triangular faces form the shape of the tip to a point. Then with a generous amount of solder paste and solder cover the entire tip, especially the triangular faces. Keep the iron at this low heat and the tip will not have to be dressed for days. Now you are ready for all soldering operations.

With a good soldering iron any number of different solders and fluxes may be used. The best tinners solder is called 50/50 because it contains equal parts of lead and tin. Due to its lower melting temperature and ease of flowing it is excellent for this type of work. A solid type of solder (bar or wire) is recommended as it is much easier to control the amount of solder and flux combination. In most cases non-corrosive paste will be a suitable flux. Rosin will not do unless the wire is cleaned very carefully after each use. Cutting acid flux may be used but requires careful cleaning of the work to prevent corrosive action later. Use solder sparingly and pull iron away from joint so as to draw off excess solder.

The flux is used on the parts to be soldered to remove the oxides which may surround and protect the metal. You can't get solder to stick to an oxide covered piece of metal there - for use flux to prepare and clean the surface. Solder is not a cement and will not adhere to the metal surface unless the metal is hot enough to permit the solder to weld onto it. The best temperature is one which permits the solder to flow freely from the iron to the joint and then congeal before it runs off again. Remember both pieces of metal to be joined must be equally hot.

By tinning we mean covering the surface of a piece of wire with solder previous to making a joint with another piece. Thus two pieces may be tinned before bringing them together to form the joint. By "tacking" we mean making a small joint, or attachment point, to hold the parts until they can be more fully joined.

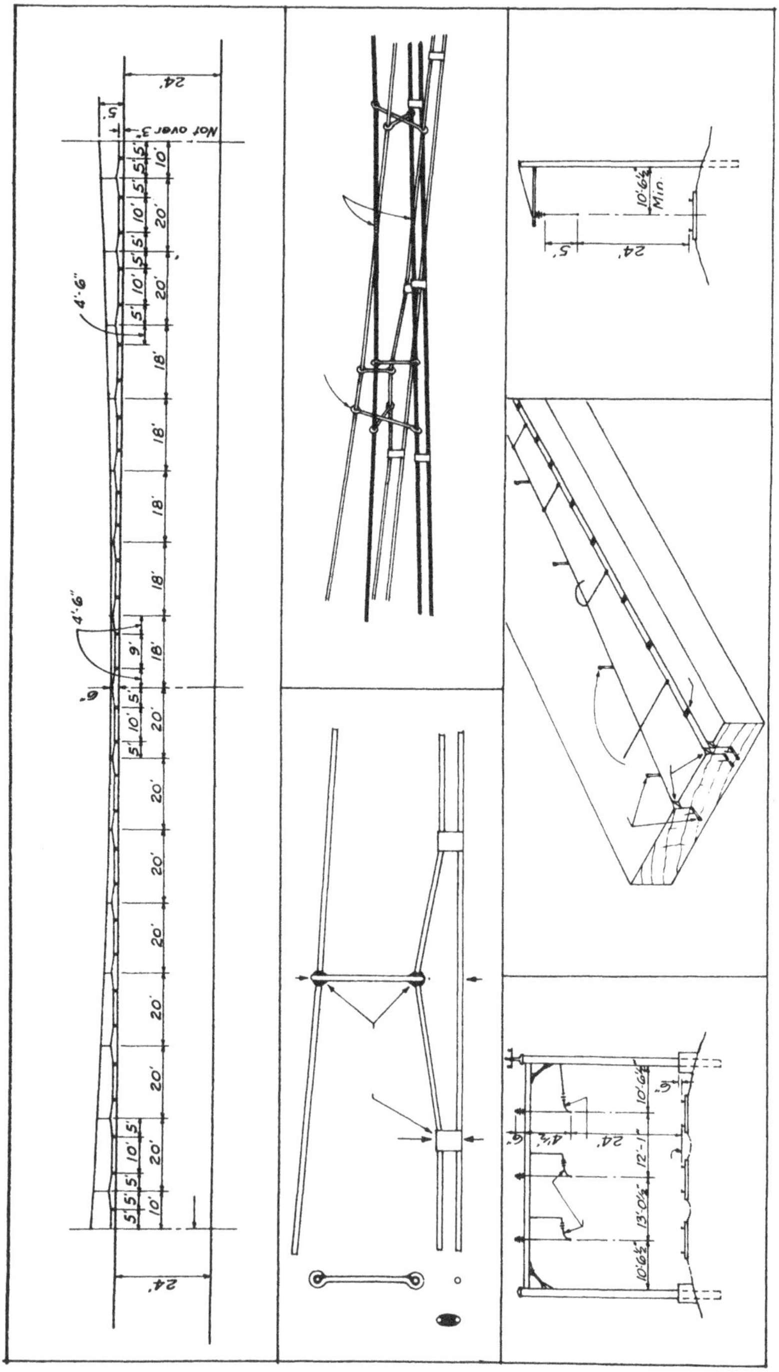

FIG. 35 METHODS FOR JIGGING FOR CATENARY CONSTRUCTION. Plan originally developed by Temple Nieter

Chapter 5

THE ELECTRIC CIRCUIT

With the Track and overhead wiring complete the next thing to provide is the electrical system with which the trolley cars will be run. This includes the power supply, the switches and rheostat for starting and stopping the cars and controlling their speed and the necessary wiring for connecting the power, controls and track together. With this will be included some devices for controlling some of the operations in an automatic manner. The subject of electrical work has been so well covered in magazine articles and books that only such details as are of pertinent operation to the trolley builder will be covered.

Your Power Supply. Whether you use direct current (DC) or alternating current (AC) will depend upon the type of motors you choose for powering your motor cars. HO scale and the other smaller scales require permanent magnet motors because this type can be made to fit a smaller space than a motor with a wound field. Permanent magnet motors can only be operated on direct current. The wound field motor used on tinplate cars and for nearly all O scale equipment can be operated on either direct or alternating current. For O cars which require a small power unit carried under the floor of the car, the permanent magnet motor is the only answer. So, before you decide on a power supply unit, determine what kind of motors you will use and the kind of power required to operate them. If in doubt

remember that any type of motor will operate on direct current but only motors with wound fields will operate on alternating current. Therefore, if in doubt, use DC.

All motors whether permanent magnet or wound field require 12 volts DC for operation. The wound field motors when operated on AC require 16 volts. This is a standard rating that applies to all makes of motors without respect to size or scale. The amount of current which a motor draws depends on the load it has to carry. The current varies from 1/2 amps. for small scale cars (HO) up to 1-1/2 amps for the large O systems where a power car and several trailers constitute the load. Since power is measured in Watts, which is the product of volts times amps, it will be seen that the amount of power required will depend directly on the number of cars running at one time and the size and type of motor used.

We can assume that the average power consumed by any one train of cars will be about 15 watts and from this can determine the size of the power plant according to the number of cars to be motorized. In addition you will have to figure on the amount of power required for lights and accessories to be operated at the same time you run your cars. For a large layout a certain amount of extra power should be included to cover losses in transmission.

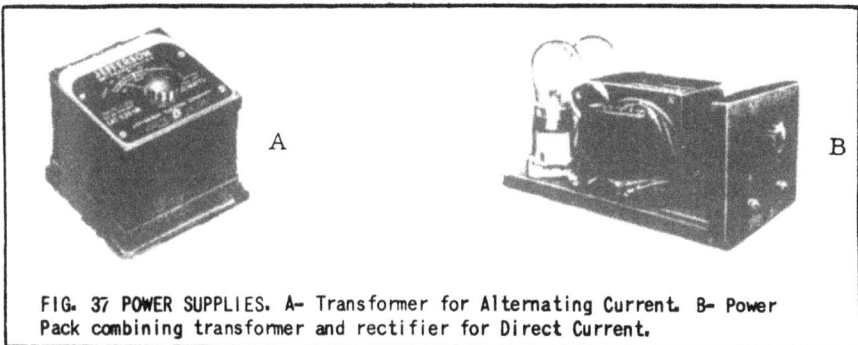

FIG. 37 POWER SUPPLIES. A- Transformer for Alternating Current. B- Power Pack combining transformer and rectifier for Direct Current.

For an alternating current powered system you use a "Transformer" for power. Today nearly all homes are wired to alternating current power lines which provide 110 volts electrical pressure. You can not use this alternating current supply for your trains directly because the voltage is 110 instead of 12 or 16. Therefore to reduce the voltage a transformer is needed. This takes the house current from the wall plug, puts it thru a coil called the "primary" and by virtue of the magnetic action inherent to an alternating current "induces" a current to flow in a "secondary" coil which is not electrically connected to the primary coil.

Another interesting phenomena connected with this transformation is that the voltage of the AC which flows from the secondary coil can be either higher or lower than the voltage applied to the primary coil.

The voltage ratio depends on the relative number of turns of wire on the primary and secondary coils. For example if we want 16 volts at the secondary and 110 volts is applied to the primary then we must have 16/110 times as many turns of wire on the secondary as on the primary. This is the fundamental principle of the transformer and why this device is so valuable in providing just the voltage required for any type of service. A transformer cannot be used with direct current and in fact there is nothing that can be used with DC that actually takes the place of a transformer.

Transformers of the toy or model type are provided with a cord and plug for connecting to the house circuit at a convenient receptacle. They also have a number of binding posts which are connected to different sections of the secondary coil so that a variety of voltages may be obtained by connecting up to the posts marked for the desired voltage. Sometimes a transformer has a sliding arm which makes contact to one of a series of contacts and by moving this arm from contact to contact the voltage is varied and serves as a speed regulator much in the manner of a rheostat.

A transformer rated at 75 watts is large enough for a small to fair sized trolley system. A 150 watt transformer will take care of a large system and a 250 size is ample for a complete system with lights and many accessories. Transformers designed for ringing bells are not large enough nor do they have the proper voltages for model service.

You frequently can find a radio type transformer that has suitable secondary voltages for lighting lights and operating accessories but most of the radio types are designed for either 2.5 or 6.3 volt outputs. Then there are the so called "signal" types of transformers which have voltage taps for 6, 12, 18 and 24 volts. These usually are rated at 250 or 500 watts. They are particularly useful for building power packs for changing AC to DC by means of a rectifier.

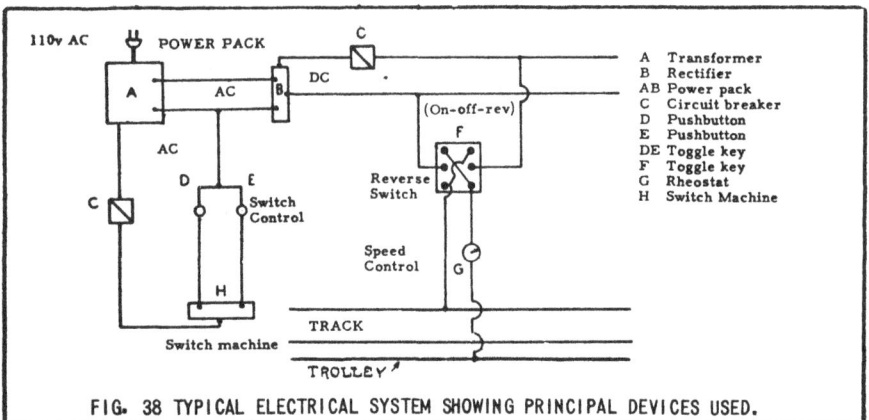

FIG. 38 TYPICAL ELECTRICAL SYSTEM SHOWING PRINCIPAL DEVICES USED.

For direct current operation you can use two 6 volt automobile storage batteries in series. Actually you will have to use three of these batteries in series because the 12 volts you get from two will not give you the extra margin you need at times for overcoming losses in your track and trolley wires. But if you do not wish to put up with storage batteries (which are messy and require frequent recharging), you use what is called a "power-pack". This is a transformer connected up to a device known as a "rectifier" and which acts as a check valve in a water line in that it changes the alternating current to direct current.

Actually, the alternating current becomes a pulsating current with all the pulsations flowing in one direction. In other words the rectifier "valves" the "plus" pulses thru one path and the "minus" pulses thru another and in the process gets both the plus and minus pulses to flow in the same direction. It sounds complicated but it is just as simple as a reciprocating pump with one way valves that open and close as the water moves back and forth but which sends the water out into the pipe line in a continuous stream.

If you already have a transformer and you want to convert to direct current you can purchase a rectifier which can be connected to the transformer to change the AC to DC. In selecting the rectifier keep in mind that the AC voltage which you put into the rectifier (imput voltage) must be double the DC voltage you desire to obtain (output voltage). The new type Selenium rectifiers require an imput voltage of 150% of the output. Thus a transformer capable of providing 24 volts when connected to a Copper Sulphite (old style) rectifier will rectify to 12 volts DC. This same transformer connected to a Selenium rectifier will rectify 24 volts to 16 volts DC.

The rectifiers used for this purpose are called "full-wave" or "bridge" types. They have four terminals, two for AC and two for DC. A wiring diagram accompanies all rectifiers and it is not difficult to connect them. The reason for this loss in voltage by rectification is twofold: First, it is the average and not the peak value of the AC voltage that appears as DC voltage and secondly there is a loss in pressure because of the internal resistance of the rectifier material. It should also be born in mind that rectifiers are only about 50% efficient and it is this loss in power which makes them normally hot.

The above explanation of power sources should be ample as the suppliers of these devices provide all the information required for their use. Also, we believe, that most people are familiar with transformers and power packs from having met with them in connection with other power applications.

Control Devices. Between the transformer or power pack and the track you will need something in the way of control equipment to start and stop the trains and regulate the

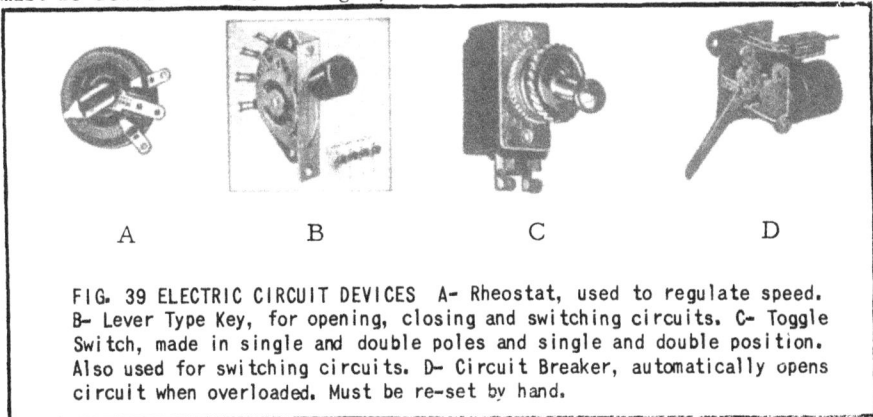

A   B   C   D

FIG. 39 ELECTRIC CIRCUIT DEVICES A- Rheostat, used to regulate speed.
B- Lever Type Key, for opening, closing and switching circuits. C- Toggle
Switch, made in single and double poles and single and double position.
Also used for switching circuits. D- Circuit Breaker, automatically opens
circuit when overloaded. Must be re-set by hand.

speed. These control devices are assembled together on a panel or board which becomes the "control board" or operating center. Along with the essential units are included lights for indicating track occupancy, buttons or keys for operating the turnout motors and switches for turning on and off any accessories located along the right-of-way.

The speed of the cars is regulated with a "Rheostat" connected in series with the power circuit (between the power supply and the track). You can, of course, regulate the speed by varying the voltage at the power supply, but it is not convenient to change wires from one binding post to another every time you wish to make the cars go faster or slower. The rheostat also varies the voltage by absorbing part of it in producing heat. In this sense it is a "waster" of electric energy in that it consumes the part which cannot be efficiently used.

Rheostats are rated two ways: in ohms resistance and watts. The resistance is a measure of the amount the voltage can be regulated and the watts indicates the current that can be safely consumed in heat. For HO systems a 30 ohm 25 watt rheostat will throttle down a train from full speed at 15 volts to a dead stop and handle up to 1 ampere without overheating. On the other hand only 15 ohms resistance is needed with O gauge systems but a 50 watt size rheostat should be used because the O gauge current runs up to 1.5 amps.

The resistance value of the rheostat must be chosen in keeping with the top voltage value from which you want to reduce to an operating value. For example, to reduce from 15 volts to 6 volts (9 volts loss) would require 18 ohms with a 1/2 amp of current flowing but only 12 ohms if the voltage had to be regulated from a high of 12 to 6 (6 volts loss). If your rheostat has too high a resistance only a small part of it will be useful whereas a rheostat with less resistance would actually be more useful because you would use a greater part of it.

For example, if you used a 30 ohm rheostat where only 15 ohms was required you would get all your speed regulation in 1/2 of the rheostat because that half would give you the full range of speeds wanted. Such a rheostat would be carrying all the current in one-half of its coil so would be over-rated. A 30 ohm rheostat rated at 25 watts will carry 1 amp. (actually .9) while a 15 ohm 25 watt rheostat will carry 1.3 amps. The carrying capacity of a rheostat in watts is determined by multiplying the resistance by the square of the current ($I^2 \times R = W$).

On the other hand if you use a rheostat with too little resistance you cannot get down to the lowest speed desired when your cars are running light. For example if your train of cars draws 3/4 amp. when loaded you can reduce the voltage from 15 to 5 with less than 15 ohms resistance but when running light and drawing only 1/2 ampere this same resistance will reduce the voltage from 15 to 7-1/2 which is not enough to get the same slow speed as if the voltage were reduced to 5. If you want to play safe you should either use a high resistance high watt rheostat to be sure you get both the speed range desired and the current carrying capacity required under the heaviest loads. Or use two rheostats and connect them either in series or parallel depending on the nature of the load and speed.

In order to determine the amount of resistance you need for any load condition you must know the maximum voltage from which the voltage must be reduced, the minimum voltage required for the slow speed, and the maximum and minimum current which the car requires at full and light loads. Since this requires so much figuring the average model operator either makes a good guess or takes the advice of his dealer. And if the first rheostat isn't right he knows what to buy the next time and finds some other use for the first one. In the end, nothing is lost.

In addition to the rheostat you will need a number of toggle switches or lever type keys for opening and closing the various sectional circuits. The number of these required

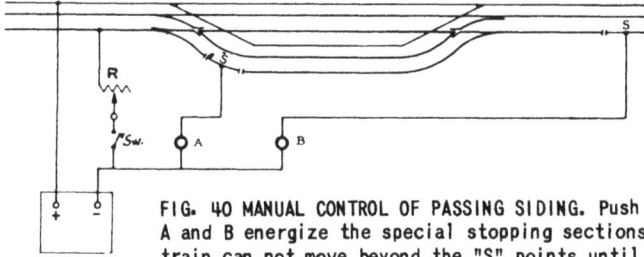

FIG. 40 MANUAL CONTROL OF PASSING SIDING. Push buttons A and B energize the special stopping sections "S". A train can not move beyond the "S" points until despatched by the operator.

will depend on how many blocks or sections you break your track system into. You can of course operate the entire system as one circuit but this will not give you much control of separate cars operated at the same time. With one control either everything is "on" or "off". Therefore it is good practice to divide the track into sections. This must be done purposefully and not indiscriminately, if you want to obtain true operation.

Take for example, the simple arrangement shown in diagram 40. This involves a straight stretch of single track with a passing siding. We desire to operate two cars, one in each direction and use the passing siding as a meeting point. The main line will represent one section and the passing siding stretch marked "S" a second. The first car leaving the east end will take the siding and come to a stop on section "S". In the mean time car number 2 is passing on the main track. As soon as no. 2 has cleared the west turnout car no. 1 can proceed.

The operator closes the circuit to section S and train no. 1 completes

its journey to the west terminal. If desired the starting of the car from section S can be made automatic upon the arrival of car no. 2 at the station marked "C", by connecting the track section of S to that of C. When C is grounded by a car passing over it the circuit to S will be complete, just as if a switch on the control board were closed by the operator.

In any long stretch of single track it is desirable to have several sections so two or more cars can follow each other and a car can be stopped in any section. A long track should have more than one passing siding so meets can be made all along the route. On a point-to-point system the terminals may diverge into several platform tracks or into a yard.

Each platform track and each yard track should have its own circuit so cars can be moved on and off each such track independent of cars on other tracks. When the track can be routed into two or more independent tracks the sections should be so chosen that any route can be controlled without interfering with another route.

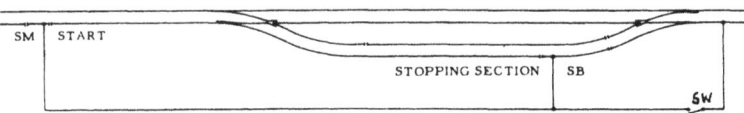

FIG. 41 AUTOMATIC CONTROL OF PASSING SIDING. Section SM on the main line is connected to section SB of the passing siding. A train stopped on the siding will be automatically restarted when another train passes over SM and completes a contact to the section SB thus completing the power to a train held on the stopping or dead part of the passing siding.

33

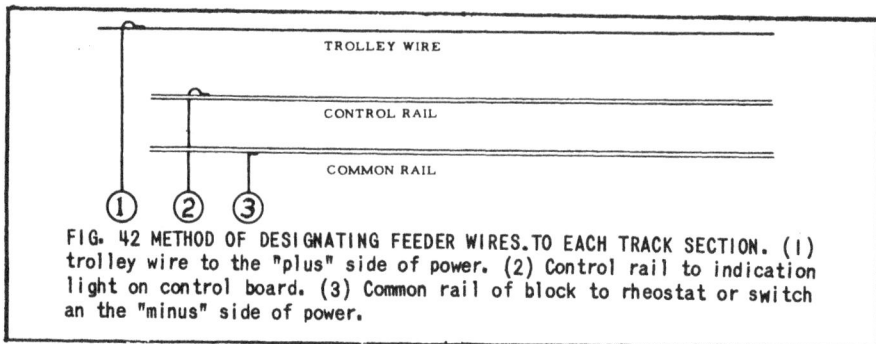

FIG. 42 METHOD OF DESIGNATING FEEDER WIRES TO EACH TRACK SECTION. (1) trolley wire to the "plus" side of power. (2) Control rail to indication light on control board. (3) Common rail of block to rheostat or switch an the "minus" side of power.

In determining how many sections to have you must take into account the size of your layout and the number of cars that will operate at the same time. There must be at least one more section, in a stretch as there will be cars operating on that stretch than there will be a section that is at all times "open". Otherwise two cars can overtake and get into the same block.

If you have several groups of sections you will require a rheostat for each group so that you can control the speed in one group without affecting another group. One group might be the main line, another the yards and terminals and still another a branch line.

The next refinement to your control board is to add indication lights which will light up whenever a car is operating in the section to which the light is connected. These lights assist the operator in controlling his cars and aid in preventing collisions. They are especially necessary for indicating tracks that cannot be seen from the control board. If you have a tunnel section be sure to provide a light for it.

If you plan to install accessories such as uncoupling ramps, crossing gates or warning signals you will need a control key for operating the circuit. Uncoupling ramps are particularly helpful in yards or on sidings where a car is to be dropped. An interesting operating proceedure can be built around the coupling and uncoupling of a car at a certain point. Perhaps part of the run requires two cars instead of one, or the diner is to be cut-off of one train and attached to another.

The operation of crossing gates and warning signals can also be done automatically by use of relays or track circuits. Let us turn now to a discussion of the wiring methods between board and track.

Wiring Methods. Starting from your power source and ending up at your track section you will have a network of wires. Unless you plan this wiring carefully it will soon get out of hand and should you ever have a fouled up circuit it will be difficult to trace if your wiring is run haphazard. In the section on overhead construction it was stated that the over head wire be laid as one continuous piece and not sectionalized. Also that the overhead wire would have to be supplied by feeder wires in order to overcome line losses. If you are using direct current connect the trolley wire (and its feeders) to the positive terminal of your power supply. There should be no rheostats or switches in this side of the circuit. In fact, this positive supply does not even have to go thru the control board except to be wired up to control and signal lights.

Before we get too deep into this wiring lets generalize a bit on what kind of wire to use and the size. For short runs (not over 25 feet) bell wire or radio hook up wire will do but for longer runs or for heavy duty at least a no. 16 wire should be used. The bell and radio wires are no. 18 and have about 1/2 the carrying capacity that no. 16 wire has. For the feeder wires use no. 14 building wire - the kind used for wiring houses.

It will also be very helpful if you

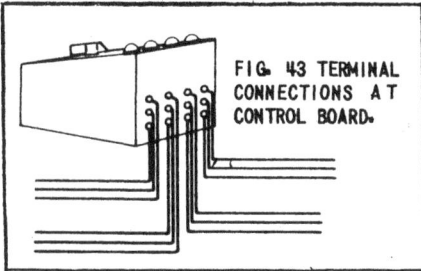

FIG. 43 TERMINAL CONNECTIONS AT CONTROL BOARD.

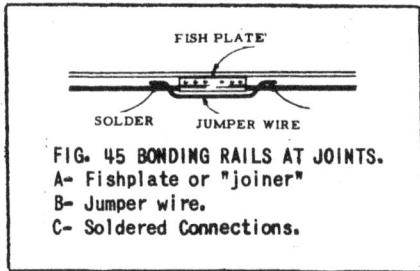

FIG. 45 BONDING RAILS AT JOINTS.
A- Fishplate or "joiner"
B- Jumper wire.
C- Soldered Connections.

use different colored wires for different kinds of circuits. The common wire which serves as a feeder should be white as white is the color used for "ground" wires on industrial and home wiring. From here on you can choose any combination of colors depending on the colors you can find. Black, white and red are the most common colors. Use the black for your track sections and the red for all special circuits. The white wire will always be the common for all circuits.

In building your control board provide a terminal board from which to take off all your connections. These terminals will connect to the switches rheostats and lights on the control board and also serve for connecting the outgoing wires to the various track sections, switch motors, coupling ramps, etc. Arrange the terminals in rows, one row for each type of circuit. Mark the terminals with numbers and make a list showing the purpose of each terminal and its circuit. For each section of track in your layout, provide two terminals one to be connected to the operating rail and the other to the control rail. The control rail terminals connect with the indication lights on the board and the operating terminals with the switches and rheostats for operating the cars. All other terminals for accessories are kept in a group by themselves.

As you run your wires out from the control center to your tracks make them up into neat cables and hold them in place with cable clamps or rings. When all your wires are strung tie the wires together by wrapping cord around the cable. On exceptionally long runs it pays to provide one or more intermediate terminal boards for the distribution of wires. By using these it is possible to build a cable of the required number of wires to a fixed point and then take off the individual connections from the terminal board. This plan keeps the wires together and also provides a means of checking and testing wires before final connection.

Whenever you make a connection to a track or trolley wire be sure to see that it is a good mechanical connection and won't come loose. If you are using some form of binding post always wind the wire on in the same direction the screw turns so that when the screw (or nut) is tightened it pulls the wire with it and not in a manner to loosen or free the wire. This is very important. There are many styles of connectors that can be used. Some of these require soldering, others crimp onto the wire. There is also a type made in two parts where each part is crimped on one of the wires to be connected, the parts are then hooked together and the joint covered with an insul-

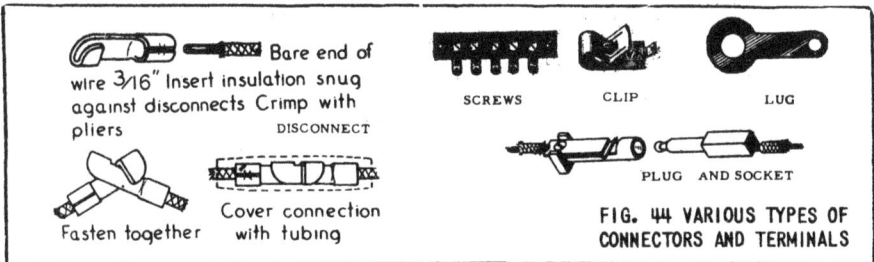

Bare end of wire 3/16" Insert insulation snug against disconnects Crimp with pliers
DISCONNECT
Fasten together
Cover connection with tubing
SCREWS   CLIP   LUG
PLUG AND SOCKET
FIG. 44 VARIOUS TYPES OF CONNECTORS AND TERMINALS

ating tubing. These are called "disconnects" because they are so easily separated again, yet hold snuggly.

If you are wiring for AC the same rules apply as for DC. The only difference is that with AC there is no plus and minus polarity, but nevertheless the two wires which carry power from the transformer must be considered as independent wires.

Reversing Motors. No provision was made on the control board for reversing the power car motors because this operation is usually performed at the car. If we are using direct current for propulsion and permanent magnet motors on the cars it would be simple to reverse the direction of running by simply reversing the polarity of the current to the rail and trolley wire. This has several disadvantages: we would either have to reverse the polarity in the entire layout or sectionalize the trolley wire so any part of the layout could be reversed without affecting other sections; if part of the trolley sections are one polarity and part another, there is always the possibility of running from one to another which would cause a short. It is better to keep the trolley wire the "plus" side of the circuit at all times and reverse the motors at the cars.

With permanent magnet motors it is only necessary to interchange the two wires which connect with the brushes because the direction of magnetism of the field remains the same and reversing the brush connections will change the direction of magnetism in the armature coils thus causing the motor to run in the opposite direction. In the case of a wound field motor, reversing the polarity to the motor will not change the direction of running because both the field and armature magnetism change direction without any relative change between them. Therefore, to reverse a wound field motor either the brush connections or the field connections are interchanged but not both.

A simple way to reverse the direction of travel of a trolley car without turning the car around is to have two trolley poles, one for each direction of running and interconnect the hooks, which hold the poles in their lowered position, with the motor circuit so that the reversing is accomplished by interchanging the trolleys. The wiring of this is shown in diagram 46. This method can also be used with a permanent magnet motor. The reversing connections can also be performed with a drum-type reversing switch or in fact any double-pole double throw toggle key or switch. Mount this inside the car so only the handle protrudes thru the side, floor or roof. Arrange the connections so the handle always points in the direction the car will move. Then you will always be able to tell which way the switch is set.

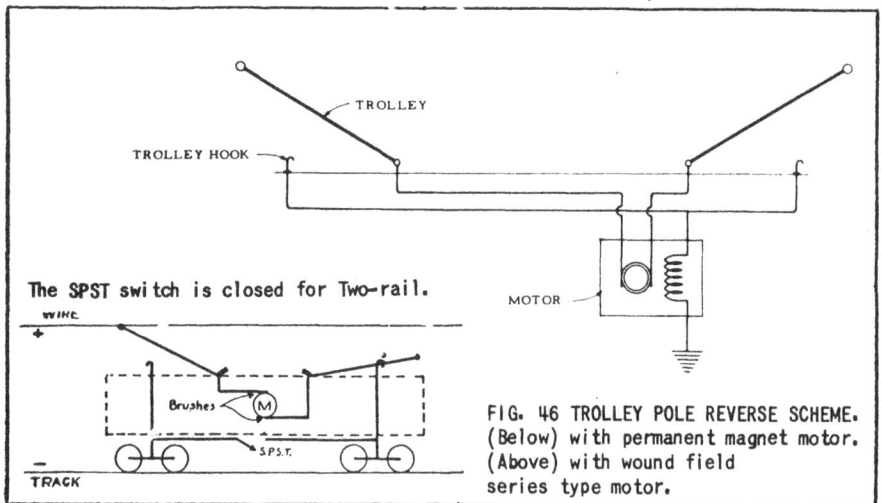

The SPST switch is closed for Two-rail.

FIG. 46 TROLLEY POLE REVERSE SCHEME. (Below) with permanent magnet motor. (Above) with wound field series type motor.

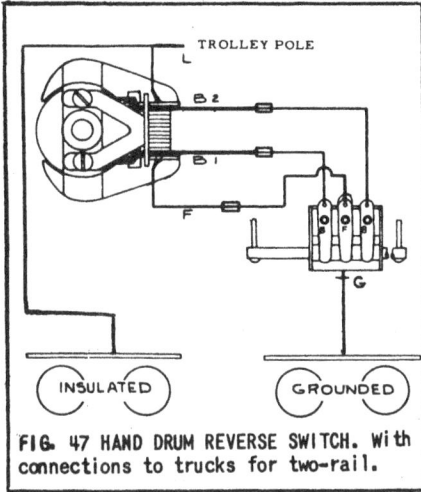

FIG. 47 HAND DRUM REVERSE SWITCH. With connections to trucks for two-rail.

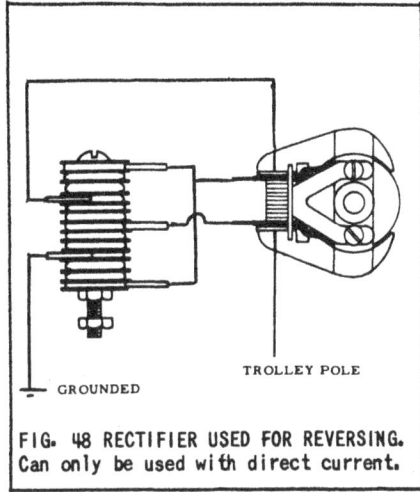

FIG. 48 RECTIFIER USED FOR REVERSING. Can only be used with direct current.

With loops at the terminals the cars are turned end for end and no other reversing is necessary. Automatic devices such as rectifiers, polarized relays and remote controlled systems such as sequence switches and selective relays which are used in steam type locomotives are not required with trolley systems but may be included on interurban systems which are to be operated more in keeping with steam or diesel propelled trains. For those who are interested in these special reversing devices we suggest a reading of one of the books on model railroad operation as space here cannot be devoted to a complete description of them.

Three-Rail and Two Rail. A trolley system is considered a three rail one since the trolley serves the purpose of the third rail. Cars built strictly for trolley line use should be constructed for three rail operation and not with insulated trucks.

This will permit three rail signalling on your trolley system. However if you are building interurban cars which may be run on a foreign system then it is better practice to insulate all trucks for two-rail operation. When running on a three rail track that is signalled, the trucks should be so placed on the car that the insulated wheels of one truck rides on one rail and that of the other on the opposite rail. Then if a wire is connected between truck bolsters the trucks will be shorted and provide a path from rail to rail by way of the uninsulated wheels and this wire. For two-rail operation the wire can be temporarily disconnected, or a slide switch provided in its circuit for opening the shorted path.

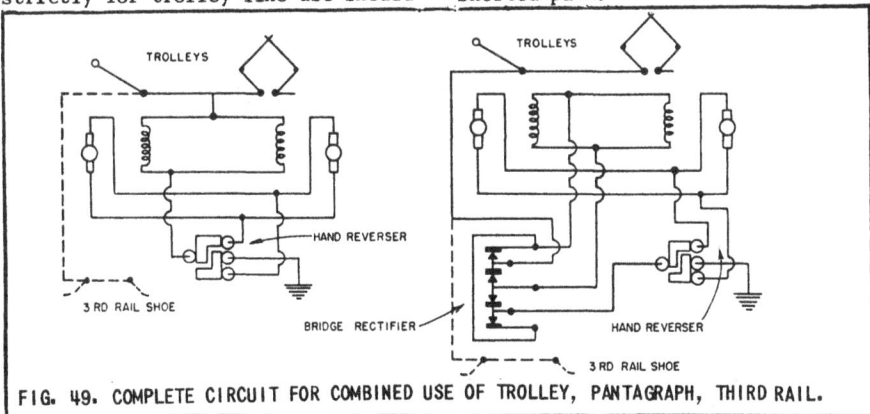

FIG. 49. COMPLETE CIRCUIT FOR COMBINED USE OF TROLLEY, PANTAGRAPH, THIRD RAIL.

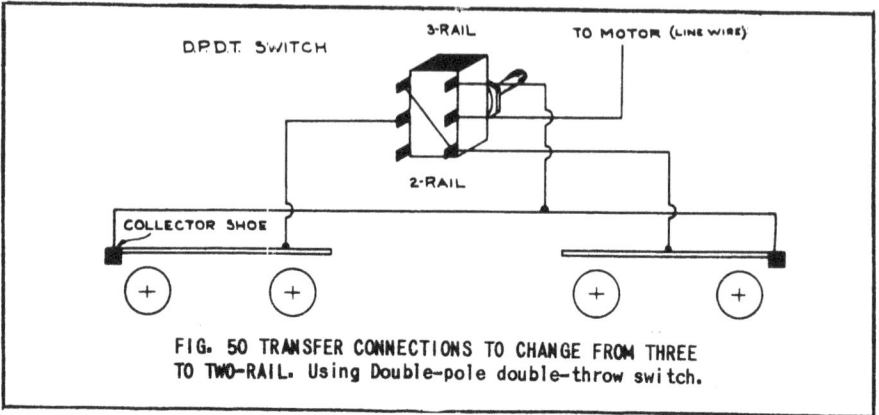

FIG. 50 TRANSFER CONNECTIONS TO CHANGE FROM THREE
TO TWO-RAIL. Using Double-pole double-throw switch.

For three-rail operation the power cars are provided with third rail pick-up shoes and these are inter-wired with the trolley circuit so that power is picked up either from the trolley or third rail. It is not necessary to have a switch in this circuit since both trolley and third rail will have the same polarity. When motors are to be run on both two and three rail tracks a switch is needed to interchange the motor connections between trucks (two-rail) and trucks and pick-ups (trolley and third-rail). This can be accomplished by a double-pole double-throw switch as shown in diagram 50.

Track Circuits. In the section on track building no mention was made of dividing up the track into control sections but this was suggested at the beginning of this section in connection with control boards and wiring. This is done for two reasons: that one section may be operated without interfering with another, and that certain signalling and protective devices can be operated by what are known as "track circuits". A track circuit is an insulated section in one of the running rails which becomes energized when the cars connect it to the other rail. When a car passes over a section

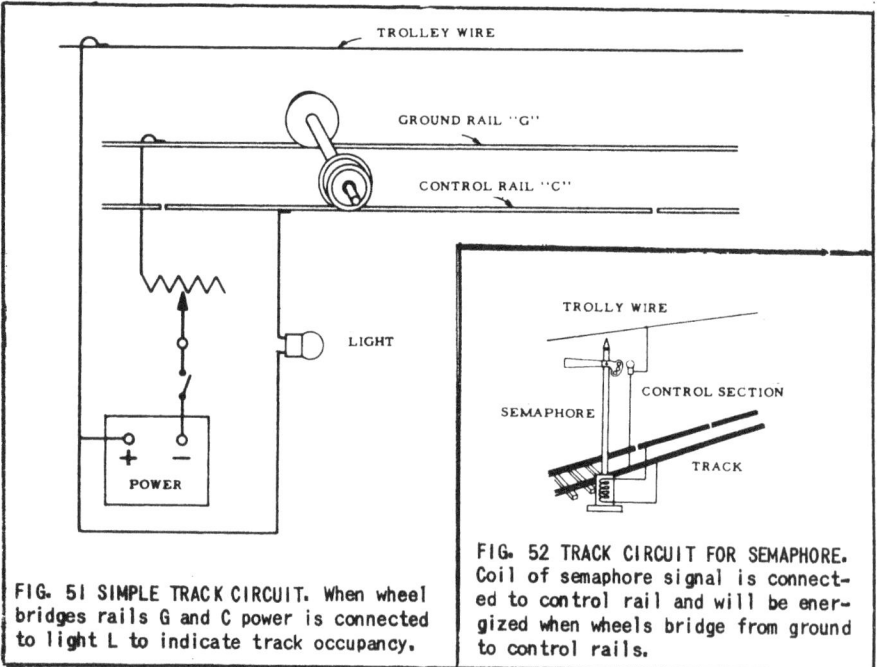

FIG. 51 SIMPLE TRACK CIRCUIT. When wheel bridges rails G and C power is connected to light L to indicate track occupancy.

FIG. 52 TRACK CIRCUIT FOR SEMAPHORE. Coil of semaphore signal is connected to control rail and will be energized when wheels bridge from ground to control rails.

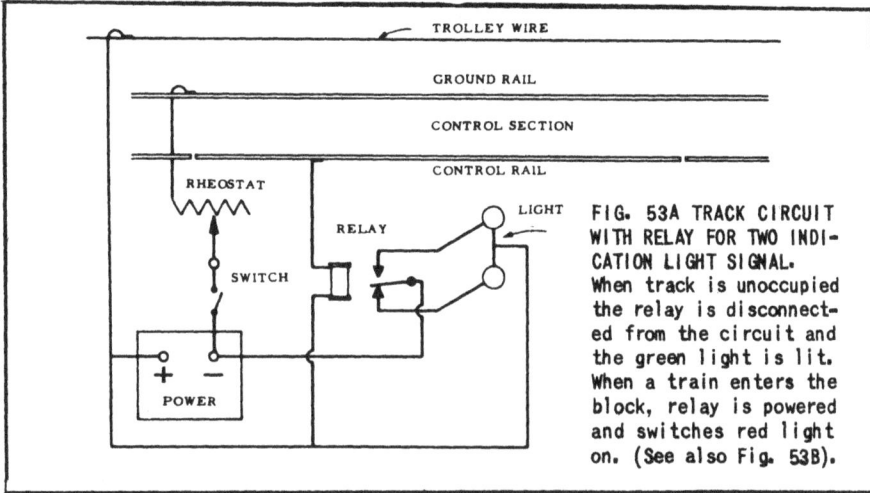

FIG. 53A TRACK CIRCUIT WITH RELAY FOR TWO INDI-CATION LIGHT SIGNAL. When track is unoccupied the relay is disconnected from the circuit and the green light is lit. When a train enters the block, relay is powered and switches red light on. (See also Fig. 53B).

such as shown in diagram 51 current is carried from the continuous rail "G" to the insulated one "C" by way of the wheels and axles of the car's truck. The action is identical to closing a switch between the two rails. Any device connected to the insulated rail will also receive power provided it has a return circuit to the power source.

The track circuit device can be used in the following ways: To light lights on the control board to show track occupancy; to operate another train as has been suggested in con-nection with a stopping track at a passing siding and to form the basis of a circuit for operating signals and providing block control protec-tion to following trains. The track circuit may also be used to operate a warning signal or lower a crossing gate at the approach of a train. This type of track circuit can only be used with a three rail system. With two-rail a relay must be con-nected in series with the track feeder wire so that any power flow-ing to the track thru this wire will energize the relay. The relay then closes the other operating circuits.

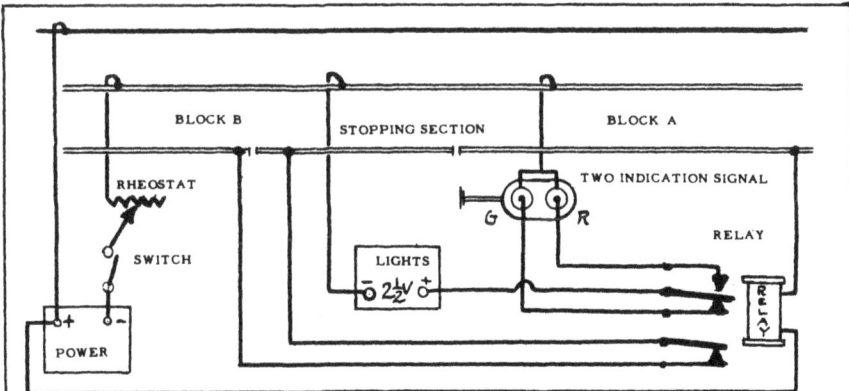

FIG. 53B TRACK CIRCUIT WITH RELAY FOR BLOCK CONTROL AND TWO INDICATION SIGNALS. This circuit is similar to that shown in Fig. 53A but includes the block control which stops a following train when a block is occupied. Two sets of springs are needed on relay, one for signals and one to control stop section. In diagram, a separate source of power is used for the low-voltage signal lamps. Diagram shows block in unoccupied. When section is occupied, relay will switch connections.

Semaphore Signal. The coil of a semaphore signal when connected to a
track circuit as shown in figure 52
will become energized when the train
operates the circuit as outlined
above. The normal de-energized position of the semaphore is at the up-
right or "clear" position. When the
car enters onto the insulated track
section and the coil is energized,
the arm assumes the vertical or
"stop" position. This is a signal to
any following train that it must
stop and not pass the signal. No
other relays are needed with this
circuit. As soon as the car passes
out of the controlling track section
the semaphore is disconnected from
the circuit and returns to its clear
position again.

Another signaling circuit is shown
in diagram 53. Here a relay connected to the insulated section of track
is energized when the car closes the
circuit. The contacts on the relay
close the circuits to the green and
red signal lights and to the protected stopping section located in
the adjacent block. The relay is no-

thing more than a double-pole double
throw toggle switch that is operated
by a magnetic coil instead of by
hand. In the normal de-energized position of the relay the light circuit is to the green light (clear)
and the circuit to the stopping section is closed to power permitting
any train to proceed over it.

When the relay is energized on the
passage of a car over its track circuit, it shifts the contacts so now
the red (stop) light is lit and the
circuit to the stopping section is
open. A following train will now
stop on reaching this section and
remain stopped until the train ahead
has moved out of the section which
operates the relay.

There are any number of interesting
control set-ups that can be worked
out with a track section of this
kind. A few added wiring diagrams
with a brief explanation are included. The reader is also referred to
other articles and books in which
he will find additional ideas and
circuiting suggestions.

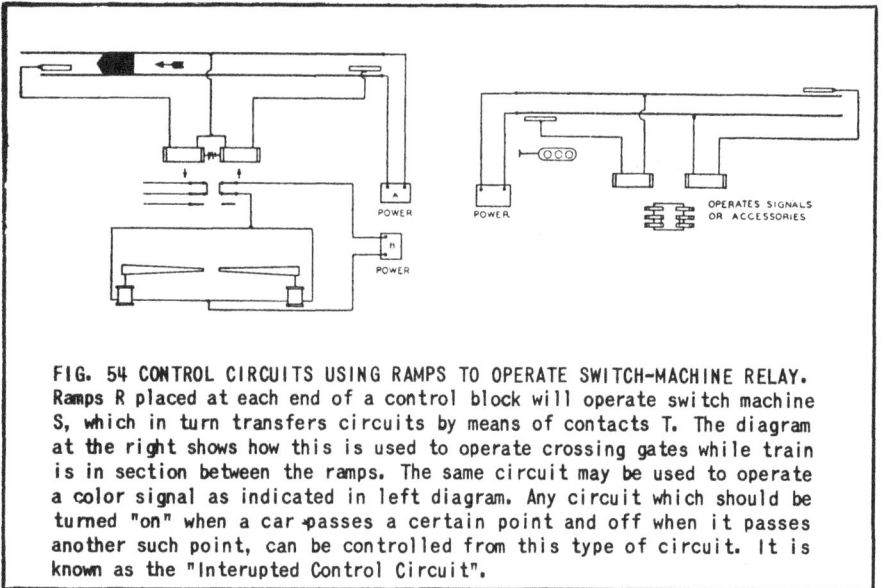

FIG. 54 CONTROL CIRCUITS USING RAMPS TO OPERATE SWITCH-MACHINE RELAY.
Ramps R placed at each end of a control block will operate switch machine
S, which in turn transfers circuits by means of contacts T. The diagram
at the right shows how this is used to operate crossing gates while train
is in section between the ramps. The same circuit may be used to operate
a color signal as indicated in left diagram. Any circuit which should be
turned "on" when a car passes a certain point and off when it passes
another such point, can be controlled from this type of circuit. It is
known as the "Interupted Control Circuit".

Chapter 6

POWER TRUCKS AND DRIVES

Today the trolley builder is offered a variety of motors and drives in all gauges. If none of these fit his particular specifications he can also build his own using motors, gears and drive parts offered by model supply houses. In this chapter we shall point out some of the more important features of the several components which go to make up a power truck and how to install and use it. For further information on any of the units described write directly to the manufacturers.

Kinds of Motors. There are three kinds of motors available to the model builder but only the smallest sizes are useful to the trolley car builder because of the limited amount of space available for the power unit. The three types are:
1. Permanent Magnet Field for use on DC only
2. Wound Field, for use on AC or DC
3. Induction Field, for use on AC only.

Permag motors, as they are familiarly called have a fixed field strength resulting from the permanently magnetized field which is in no way dependent upon the electric circuit propelling the motor. Because of their strong constant field they operate at nearly constant speed regardless of the load. It is for this reason that they start and stop suddenly. Their ability to start a heavy load is less than that of a series type wound field motor. The direction of running, of a permag motor is easy to reverse by merely changing the wires between brush connections, or reversing the wires that supply the track.

Permag motors have one advantage over other types in that they are smaller, for an equivalent output, than other types. For this reason they have found almost universal acceptance in the smaller gauges. (TT, HO and OO) where size is restricted.

The series type wound field motor is sometimes described as a "Universal" motor because it is the only type that operates equally well on direct or alternating current. Since the field is in series with the armature the same current flows thru both and since the amount of current is proportional to the load, the field strength is also in proportional to the load. Thus the speed will be slow when the field strength is greatest and will increase as the field tapers off. This characteristic is most useful in a traction motor because it makes for smooth starting and high torque under load. This type of motor will start a load that would stall an equally powered permag motor.

FIG. 55 PITTMAN MOTORS. (Upper left) DC-60, (upper right) DC-71 and 91 permanent magnet types; (lower left) AC-92 and AC-93 wound field types for AC or DC; (lower right) DC-94 and DC-95 permanent field types for DC only.

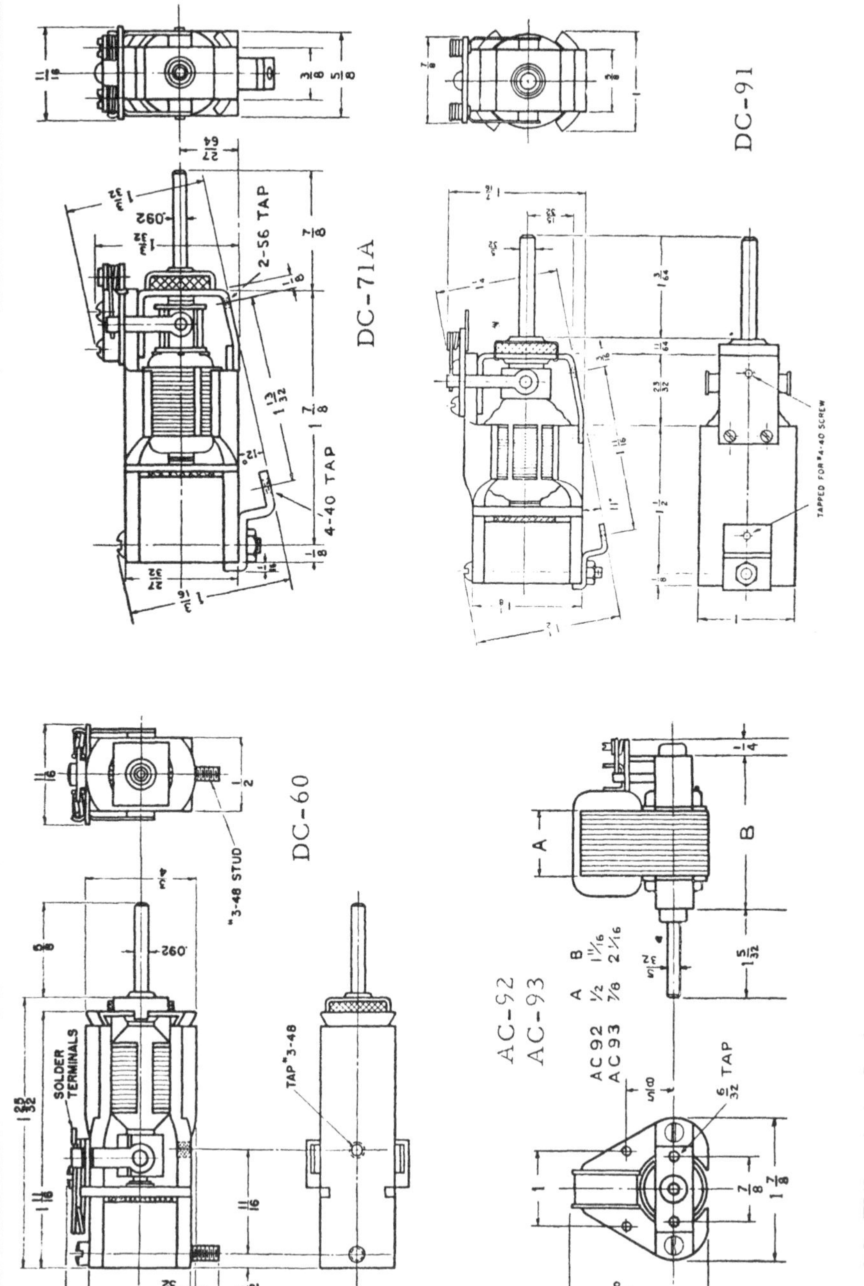

FIG. 58 DIMENSIONS OF PITTMAN DC AND AC MOTORS.

MFG.	GA.	NO.	FIELD	SPEED	AMPS	POLES	SHAFT	H.P.
\multicolumn{9}{c}{FIG. 57 CHART SHOWING MOTOR CHARACTERISTICS.}
P	HO	DC60	PM	10,000	0.6	5	3/32"	.002
P	HO	DC71A	PM	9,000	0.8	5	3/32"	.005
P	S,O	DC91	PM	6,000	1.3	7	5/32"	.009
P	O	DC92	PM	5,750	1.2	7	5/32"	.008
P	O	DC93	PM	5,000	2.2	7	5/32"	.014
P	O	AC94	WF	4,000	2.2	7	5/32"	.006
P	O	AC95	WF	4,000	3.0	7	5/32"	.009
KD	O	117-1	WF	3,100	2.1	7	3/16"	.010
KD	O	117-2	WF	3,500	3.0	7	3/16"	.020
KD	O	117-3	WF	4,000	3.5	7	3/16"	.030
KD	O	117-4	WF	4,500	4.0	7	3/16"	.040

P = PITTMAN,   KD = KENDRICK & DAVIS,   PM = PERMANENT MAGNET
WF = WOUND FIELD,   SPEED = REC. OPERATING,   AMPS = MAX SAFE.

In order to reverse a series wound field motor it is necessary to interchange either the field or the armature connections and not both. In other words the direction of current flow must be changed for either the field or the armature since changing both does not bring about a relative change between them. Therefore reversing the power leads will not change the direction of running as it will in the case of a permag motor. Reversing may be accomplished with a DPDT switch or drum controller operated by hand or one of the remote control devices (sequence switch, polarized relay, rectifier) selected according to the current (AC or DC) used for propulsion.

Series wound field motors have always been popular in the larger gauge (O) where space was available to mount them. The particular type made by Kendrick and Davis has been in use for more than 25 years. Lately other manufacturers have brought out competing motors but since these all have the same general characteristics a description of the characteristics of one will apply to all.

Motors of the induction type will operate only on alternating current and since they are not reversible are not much good for traction purposes. Their power output is below that of the other two types mentioned especially on starting under load. Motors of this type are suitable for operating accessories. Mention of this type is made here only to identify them and to point out their limitations for use in model trolley building. Induction motors have a rather wide use for operating fans, small pumps, and any type of machinery that starts readily.

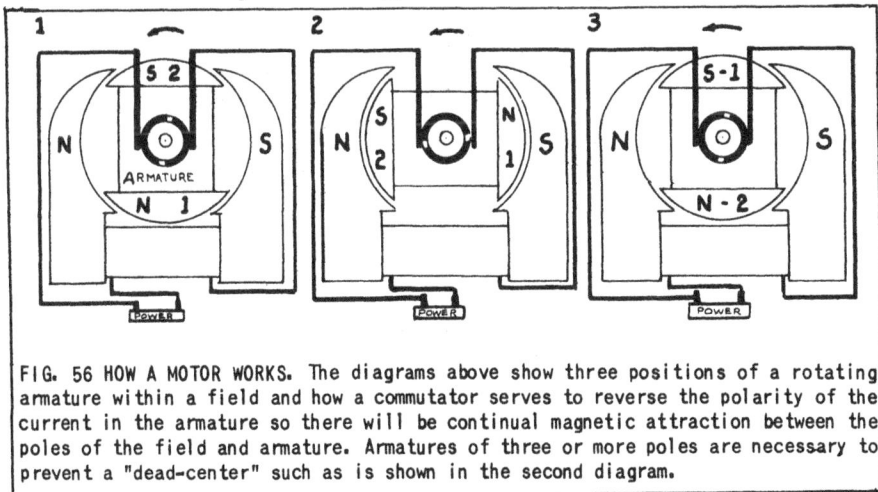

FIG. 56 HOW A MOTOR WORKS. The diagrams above show three positions of a rotating armature within a field and how a commutator serves to reverse the polarity of the current in the armature so there will be continual magnetic attraction between the poles of the field and armature. Armatures of three or more poles are necessary to prevent a "dead-center" such as is shown in the second diagram.

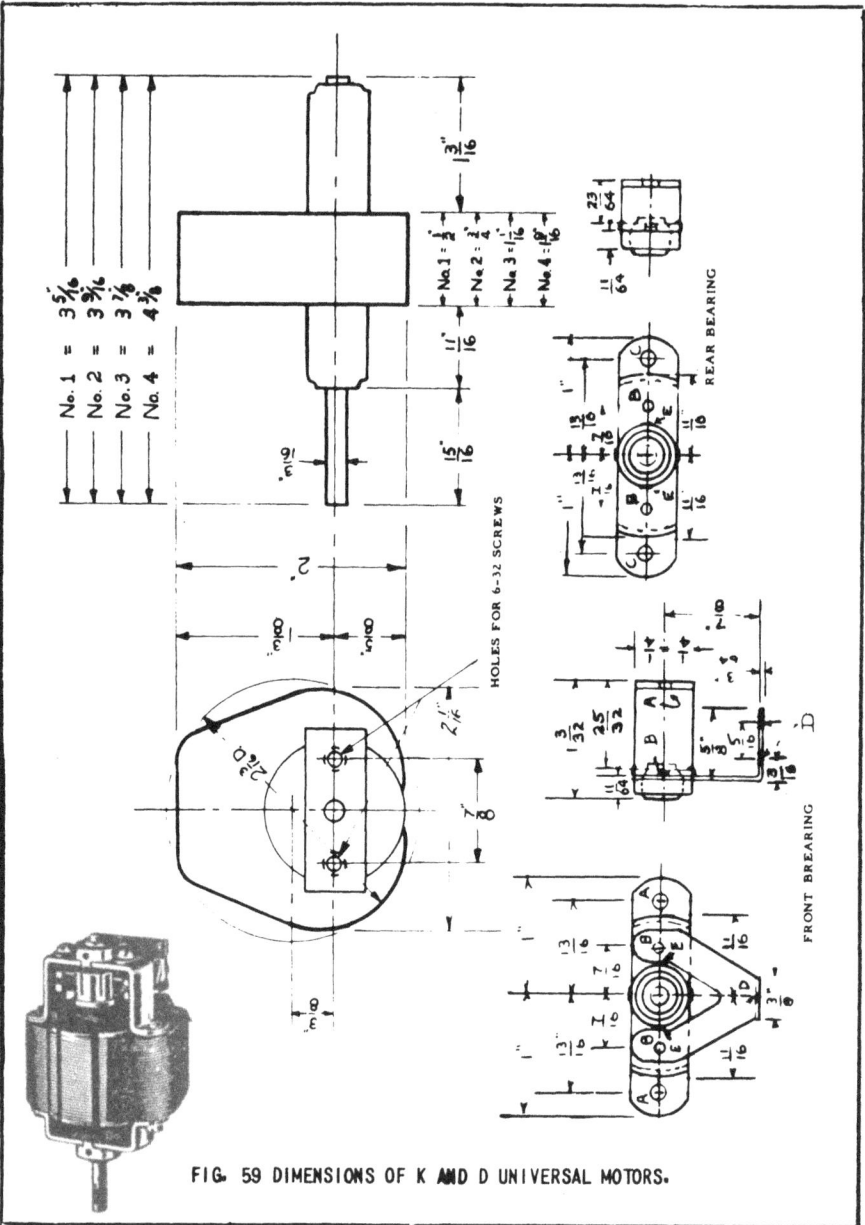

FIG. 59 DIMENSIONS OF K AND D UNIVERSAL MOTORS.

General Characteristics of Interest. Most miniature motors (permag and series wound field types) have but two poles in their field structure but may have three, five, seven or more in their armature. For each armature "pole" there will also be one segment on the commutator. A motor with only two armature poles would have a dead center from which there would be no mutual attraction be- tween field and armature to cause further rotation. Therefore at least three poles on the armature are needed and any odd number greater than three improves the running qualities. However, this last statement should be further restricted by stating that with too many poles the commutator segments would be too narrow for good commutation, so a compromise figure is always best.

For sparkless commutation the brushes must be set at a point representing the magnetic neutral between the field poles. Because of the odd number of segments on the commutator it is not possible to so locate the brushes that the motor will run equally well in either direction. As a result the motor usually runs faster in one direction. This objection could be overcome if it were practical to shift the brushes slightly when reversing the motor.

Most small motors are now equipped with impregnated bearings which are called "oil-less" bearings, but actually they do require periodic oiling for best operation. No oil should be put on the commutator but the commutator should be kept clean by washing with carbon tetrachloride and if roughened, smoothed by application of very fine sandpaper. The brushes should be fitted to the commutator so they contact the entire surface and not just along the edge. This will keep arcing to a minimum.

Before placing any motor in service see that the armature revolves freely between the pole pieces and does not rub or bind. Also check the "end-play" of the shaft. The magnetic field tends to center the armature (laterly) when rotating. If the armature presses against either bearing, when running, remove one of the end brackets and by adding or subtracting washers which are placed between the armature and bearing, align the armature so it will run freely. You will find that washers are already assembled to the armature shaft for this purpose.

If you are using a series wound motor check the connections to be sure that the field is connected in series with the armature and not in parallel with it. This, incidentally, is an error which is very frequently made. If the field and armature are connected in parallel (as a shunt type motor), the motor will run slow and overheat on even a small load. If you will follow these suggestions you will get better service from your motor and insure its faithful operation.

Motor Chart and Dimensions. In selecting a motor for a certain installation it is necessary to know its overall size, the voltage and current it takes to operate, and dimensions pertaining to mounting, shaft diameters, etc. The diagrams list the important characteristics of motors suitable for trolley car use. Dimensions are given for motors manufactured by Pittman, Kendrick and Davis and Multi-Unit. While these are not the only small motors made, they are representative of this class and constitute the ones most readily available.

Pittman built motors are made in two styles: the DC 60, 71 and 91 are of the "tunnel" type, long and narrow in dimension. The DC94 and DC95 and AC94 and AC95 follow the usual bi-polar construction lines. The AC and DC types are interchangeable, number for number. The mounting holes in these last four mentioned motors are the same as for the K and D types. Pittman motors are longer and narrower than the corresponding K and D sizes.

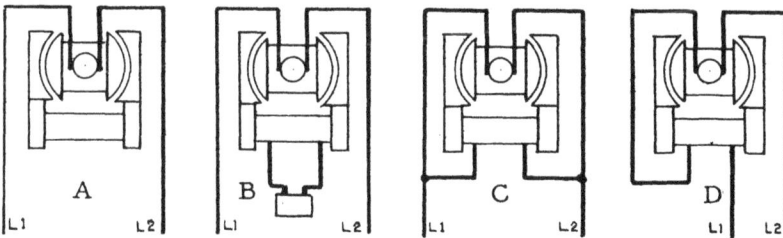

FIG. 60, DIFFERENT WAYS OF CONNECTING MOTOR ARMATURE AND FIELD. A- Permanent Magnet B- Self Excited Field, C- Shunt, D-Series. The P-M type is used only on DC propelled roads. The series type offers the greatest starting pull therefore is preferred for traction purposes. The other two types are seldom used in model traction cars.

There are four sizes of motors in the K and D line all having the same cross sectional dimensions but varying in length. All of these motors are 2-1/16" wide and all can be enclosed in a circle of 2-3/16". The center of this enclosing circle is 3/8" back from the center of the shaft. The shaft diameter of all K and D motors is 3/16" while that of the Pittman motors is 5/32". Any gears made to fit one of these motors will either have to be drilled or bushed to fit the other.

The Multi-Unit motor is unique in that it is a self contained traction motor complete with gears and wheels and of a size which permits it to be included is part of a standard truck (O gauge) for under floor mounting. Either one or two can be used in a truck. With one motor per truck, the king pin of the truck should be shifted closer to the center of the motor so the weight of the car will be over the motor. With two motors per truck this is not necessary. Only one size of this motor is being manufactured at this time.

The Multi-Unit motor is a series wound type suitable for use on either AC or DC. Its self contained gears have a ratio of approximately 15:1 and with this gearing runs at a suitable speed. One of these motors will pull a single car but two are required if a trailer is to be pulled. It takes four of these motors per power car to equal the tractive effort of the larger motors.

The chart will give you the comparitive rating of the various motors shown. These are the ratings and figures supplied by the manufacturers and have not been verified. All of these motors will operate on 12 volts direct current. The wound field types will operate on 16 volts alternating current. It should be noted that it requires 25% higher voltage for AC operation than for DC to obtain the same speed and power output. Motors run just as smoothly and are just as powerful on AC as they do on DC but their efficiency on AC is slightly less. This means it takes more power imput to get the same output but since the

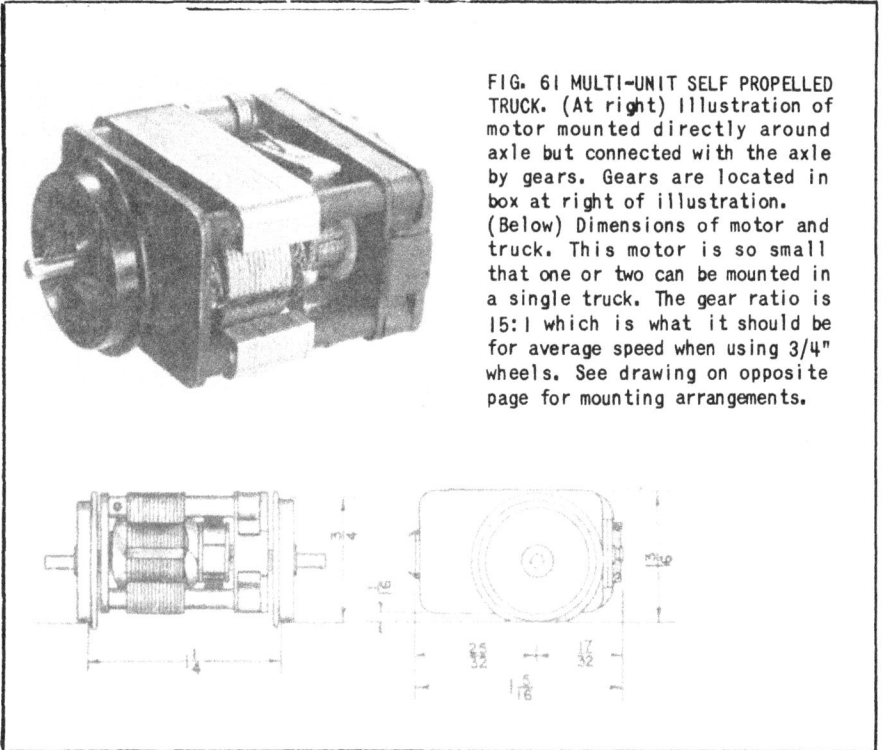

FIG. 61 MULTI-UNIT SELF PROPELLED TRUCK. (At right) Illustration of motor mounted directly around axle but connected with the axle by gears. Gears are located in box at right of illustration.
(Below) Dimensions of motor and truck. This motor is so small that one or two can be mounted in a single truck. The gear ratio is 15:1 which is what it should be for average speed when using 3/4" wheels. See drawing on opposite page for mounting arrangements.

cost of electricity is not an important item in trolley operation, this is of no particular concern.

Do not use a larger motor than recommended just because it has more power than a smaller one. It is not the power of the motor that counts but the power that can be utilized in tractive effort. If the wheels of your car slip it means you are forcing the motor to do more than the car can use. Adding weight will increase traction if the weight is properly placed over the power truck. An oversize motor uses more electricity in doing the same work a smaller motor will do efficiently.

Transmission Methods. In the last fifteen years there has been a continuous evolution of gear boxes and transmission drives as different manufacturers have attempted the problem of developing a small self contained motorized truck for trolley car propulsion. It has been a question of getting maximum rotatability, satisfactory motor mounting and proper disposition of the motor

itself. Cost, too, is important as well as gear ratios, side frames and other details. It might be interesting to review some of the methods used and while all of them are no longer commercially available, any can be duplicated by the builder.

The earliest drive that the writer can remember used a train of spur gears to connect the motor shaft (the motor was set crosswise) to the wheels. This was used by Voltamp, Carlisle and Finch, Lionel and others. Pittman has used this same method on some of his late trolley power trucks. It requires many gears to get a suitable power reduction and the arrangement is suitable only to motors with short armatures that can be mounted crosswise. Such a power truck is bulky and is apt to be noisier than other types.

Next, bevel gears were introduced so the motor could be mounted lengthwise in the car body and power transmitted by two sets of bevel gears, one to change the motion from horizontal to vertical and the other to return it from vertical to horizon-

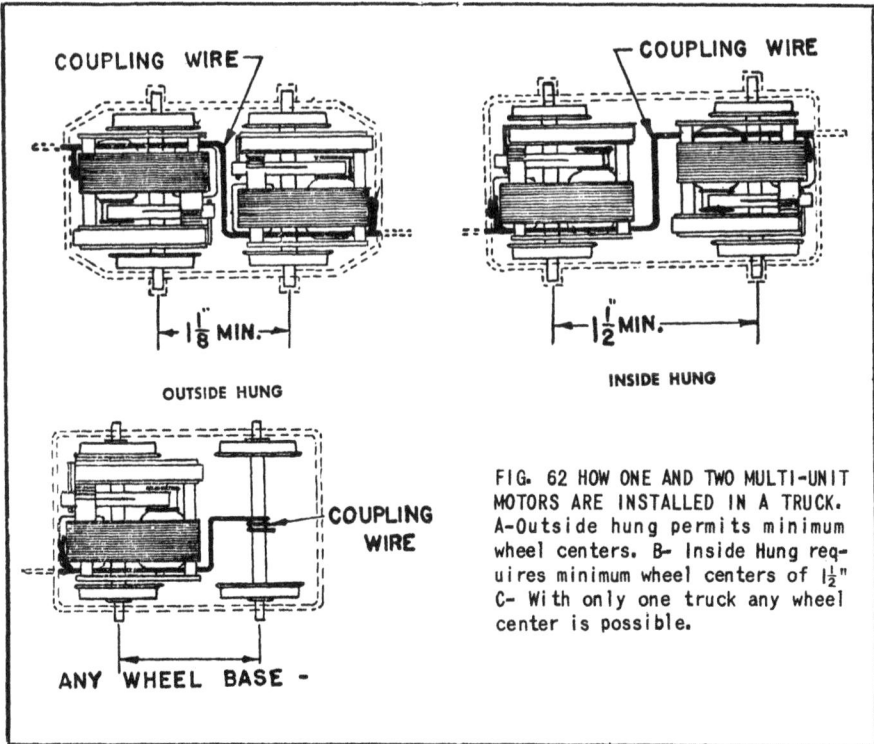

FIG. 62 HOW ONE AND TWO MULTI-UNIT MOTORS ARE INSTALLED IN A TRUCK. A-Outside hung permits minimum wheel centers. B- Inside Hung requires minimum wheel centers of 1½" C- With only one truck any wheel center is possible.

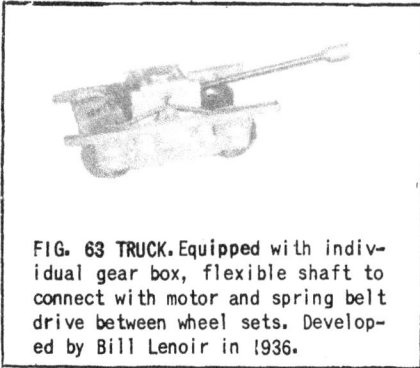

FIG. 63 TRUCK. Equipped with individual gear box, flexible shaft to connect with motor and spring belt drive between wheel sets. Developed by Bill Lenoir in 1936.

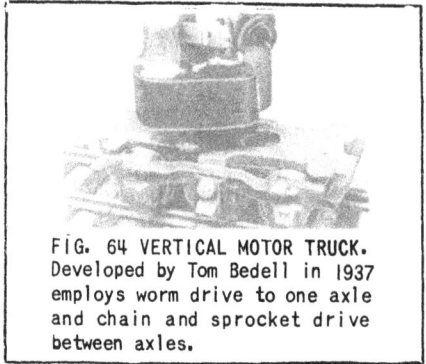

FIG. 64 VERTICAL MOTOR TRUCK. Developed by Tom Bedell in 1937 employs worm drive to one axle and chain and sprocket drive between axles.

tal. The vertical power shaft had to serve as the truck's king pin and this required a special mounting arrangement, with a bushing to enclose the rotating power drive shaft. This construction was expensive and required a lot of fussy work to get it satisfactorily mounted. In order to get sufficient speed reduction the bevel gears had to be large or other gears were needed to get the overall reduction ratio. Bevel gear methods soon passed out of popularity.

About this time Bill Lenore (an old trolley fan) came up with an idea of a simple gear box that could be mounted on the truck axle and driven thru a flexible shaft from a motor mounted centrally in the car body. By placing the motor on a special bracket located at the car's midpoint, and adding a jack shaft, it was possible to drive both trucks from the same motor. The jack shaft with its double extension was driven

from the motor shaft by a pair of spur gears. This provided a greater overall speed reduction and also made it possible to vary the speed by using different spur gear arrangements.

Since only one axle on each truck could be directly driven in this manner, the second axle was connected to the first by a spring belt running over pulleys cut on the inner face of the driving wheels. This was a very flexible arrangement and the trucks were in no way rigid. This drive was applied to the first North Shore cars (O gauge) built by Walthers. It was superceeded about 1940 by an integral truck unit which was more adaptable to other types of interurban cars. It was shown that the spring drive was not too satisfactory as slippage, to a high degree, developed when the springs stretched, pulleys were worn smooth and dirt and oil accumulated.

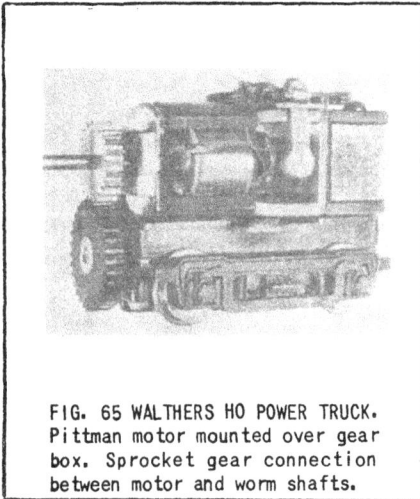

FIG. 65 WALTHERS HO POWER TRUCK. Pittman motor mounted over gear box. Sprocket gear connection between motor and worm shafts.

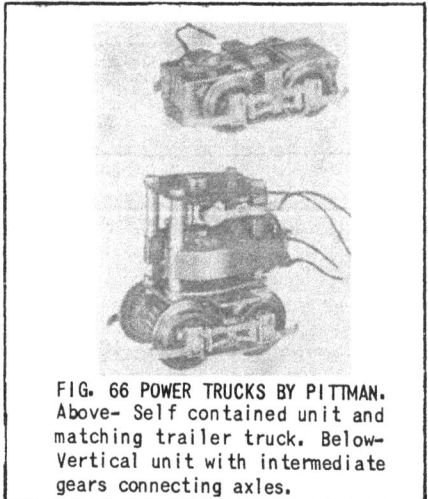

FIG. 66 POWER TRUCKS BY PITTMAN. Above- Self contained unit and matching trailer truck. Below- Vertical unit with intermediate gears connecting axles.

In order to drive two or more axles from the same motor the horizontal gear box came into use. This consisted of a worm shaft driven from a motor mounted horizontally above the box, and driving worm gears on the wheel axles. This design called for rigidly mounted axles, without springing action, and therefore had to be carefully built to insure contact of all wheels with the rail. The motor and worm shafts were connected by spur gears, where space permitted their use, or with pulleys and a spring or rubber belt. This particular design has been applied to power trucks of all gauges and has been found especially satisfactory for the smaller sizes. Each manufacturer who makes this style of truck has incorporated his own features but all trucks are only as good as their motors.

About 1935 Tom. Bedell brought out a motorized truck for his O gauge New Haven switcher in which the motor was mounted vertically and connected to one of the axles by a worm and gear set. The second axle was driven from the first by a small ladder chain operating over sprockets. All wheels were flexible and powered and the unit was compact and simple to mount with maximum rotatability. Much criticism was offered against this drive because the motor was vertical instead of horizontal, and that the chain would be noisy. Mr. Bedell overcame all these objections. K and D redesigned their motor with bearings that could be run vertically and Boston Gear Co. offered a high tensile steel chain that would not stretch under wear and would run quiet. The best proof to all of this is that units built 15 years ago are still giving satisfactory service.

Whatever choice of power truck, or transmission method you make, you may be sure that it will have both good and bad points all depending on what you expect from it. We would like to summarize on the advantages and disadvantages of the different types, as we appraise them. The horizontally mounted motor will give less rotatability than the vertical motor, but the latter is restricted in length that can be accomodated under the roof of the car.

All gear drives are noisy but sometimes the fault lies with a motor that "whines". Adding a good grease like "Lubriplate", will help greatly in reducing gear and chain noises. Avoid spring drives where motor shafts are small in diameter as the spring tension will tend to bend the shaft. If you must keep your entire power plant under the floor of your car do not expect the same power from a smaller motor that you would get from a larger one. Do not hesitate to use motors that are labeled for one gauge on another if they serve your purpose. Such gauge labels have nothing restrictive about them because all motors now operate under the same voltage and circuits.

We have shown on these pages illustrations of as many different styles of power trucks as we could and give a brief mention of each with the illustration. Not all of these are being marketed today and some were "war babies" that were made available only because more satisfactory material could not be had at the time. There have been several excellent articles published telling how to build a motor truck. Consult these if you wish to start from scratch.

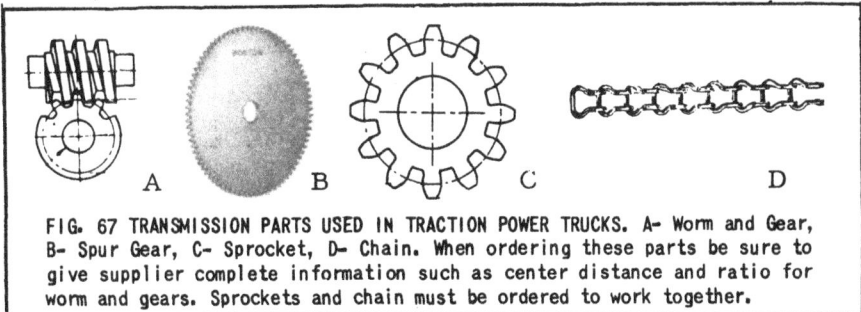

FIG. 67 TRANSMISSION PARTS USED IN TRACTION POWER TRUCKS. A- Worm and Gear, B- Spur Gear, C- Sprocket, D- Chain. When ordering these parts be sure to give supplier complete information such as center distance and ratio for worm and gears. Sprockets and chain must be ordered to work together.

Gear Ratios and How to Figure Them.
In order to find out how many gears and what ratio to use in reducing the speed of the motor to that of the wheels, the following information is needed: speed of motor, diameter of wheel and scale speed desired. First determine the number of revolutions the drivers should make per minute in order to run at the proper scale speed, then divide this number into the number of revolutions the motor makes per minute and the quotient will be the ratio for the gearing.

Let's take an example to see how this computation works out. Assume a driver diameter of one inch and a scale speed of 60 miles per hour or one mile per minute. In 1/4" scale, a scale mile is equal to 110 feet or 1320 inches. A one inch driver has a circumference of 3.1416 inches. The number of revolutions is the quotient of these figures (1320 ÷ 3.1416 = 420) or 420 per minute. If we take the average motor speed to be about 6400 rpm the required ratio will be 16:1. Since there are 16 sixteenths in an inch, we can establish an interesting way to remember how to figure gear ratios.

In other words, in O gauge (1/4" scale) we can figure on one point in the gear ratio for every 16th in the diameter of the driver. For HO gauge it would be one half of this or 1/32", for S gauge 3/64", etc. This

is an easy way to figure gear ratios, and is sufficiently close to give the right scale speed.

For other scale speeds it is only necessary to work out a proportionate ratio according to how much faster or slower the desired speed is to the base figure for a 60 mile per hour speed. For example, for freight service slower running is desirable so the gear ratio must be increased. The table (figure 67) gives the ratios for freight (45 miles per hr.), passenger (60 mph) and streamlined (90 mph) operation. This table is based on a motor speed of 6500 rpm. For other wheel diameters and motor speeds it is only necessary to interpolate the figures given and proportion the ratio in keeping with the motor speeds. Remember, that the faster the motor runs the higher must be the gear ratio, everything else remaining the same.

The gear ratios which manufacturers apply to their trucks is usually about right allowing for the different types of service to be covered. If the ratio is too high (speed too low) it prevents obtaining a higher speed without increasing the voltage above a safe level for the motor. On the other hand if the ratio is low (speed too high) a reduction in speed is possible by introducing resistance in the propulsion circuit.

GEAR RATIOS - For All Scales				
Figured for a motor speed of 6500 revolutions per minute.				
Wheel Diam.	Switcher 30 m.p.h.	Freight 45 m.p.h.	Passenger 60 m.p.h.	Streamliner 90 m.p.h.
20"	13:1	10:1	6:1	4:1
22"	15:1	11:1	7:1	5:1
24"	16:1	12:1	8:1	6:1
26"	18:1	14:1	9:1	7:1
33"	22:1	16:1	11:1	8:1
36"	24:1	18:1	12:1	9:1
48"	32:1	24:1	16:1	12:1
Gear ratios for all scales are the same for each wheel size as scale reductions for wheel size and scale speed remain constant.				
For motors running around 10,000 r.p.m. the gear ratios should be 50% higher to obtain same wheel r.p.m.				

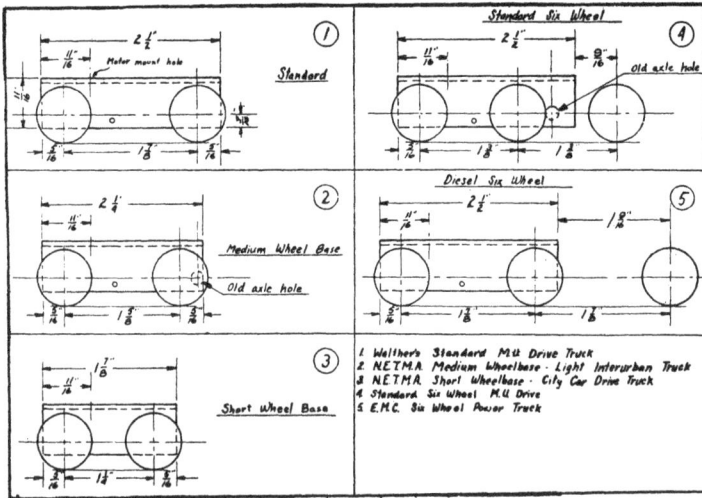

FIG. 68 WHEEL ARRANGEMENTS. See text this page for further details.

Wheel Bases and Side Frames. Most trucks are built to be used with a limited number of side frames with a fixed wheel base. Since the side frames are not needed for bearings it is possible to hang the side frames on so they over or underhang the wheel base. If the difference is slight this will not be too apparent to the eye. With a gear box of the channel type using a chain drive between axles it is possible to remount one of the axles and thereby reduce the wheel base or adopt a four wheel truck to a six wheel design. How this can be done with some types of construction is shown in diagram 68.

Motor Mounting Methods. Most motors are provided with screw holes for mounting the motor to the truck frame and some are provided with special brackets for this purpose.

The bearing brackets of K and D and Pittman Motors (94 and 95 frames) are drilled for 6/32 screws at 7/8" centers.

The manner of mounting the truck to the car body determines its rotatability or pivoting angle. To obtain the greatest amount of swing, the pivot point should be placed as close to the center of the motor as possible. The motor truck should be able to turn at least 15^0 from each side or 30^0 in all. More swing is needed for trolley trucks operating on the smaller radii. The bracket on which the truck pivots should preferably be attached to the car floor, either to the front, back or side. The truck attachment should be as low as possible. When the bracket is attached to the roof of the car as were some of the older Z brackets and snap arrangements, the motor

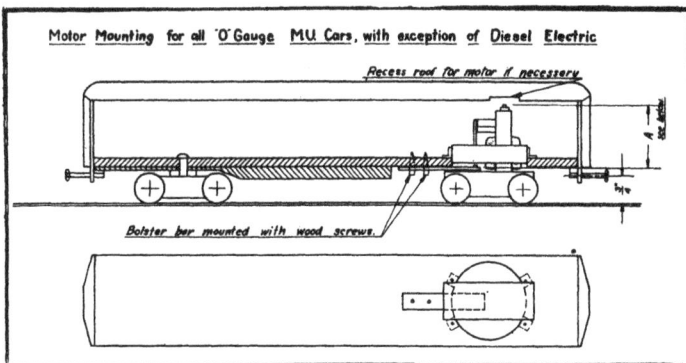

FIG. 69 RING MOUNTING FOR motor suspension.

will jerk and tilt the truck on starting frequently causing a derailment. The bracket and ring scheme shown in figure 69 works out nicely for K and D motors. The inside diameter of the ring or sleeve must be 2-3/16". The sleeve should be made of brass and cut open at one point so it does not build up eddy currents from its closeness to the motor field. This applies only when the motor is operated by AC.

Side Frames. The number of different side frames available from any one source is rather limited. The builder will in many cases have to provide his own style or make them up from scratch. Illustrations of some of the more popular types of frames are shown in figure 70.

Most power trucks are made with inside bearings so the side frame is not required to have bearing holes for the axles. This simplifies the attachment of the side frame. Holes are usually provided in the gear box or main frame of the truck for use in fastening the side frames. By using 2-56 screws and cutting off the head, the frames may be secured by turning one end of the screw into the side frame and attaching the

other end to the hole in the gear box or channel by nuts inside and outside of the box wall. Or, if the side frames are to be suspended as dummies, the protruding ends of the axles can be cut off and the frames attached by running a small screw thru the frame and into a tapped hole in the gear box using washers to space out the frame from the channel. The head of the screw should be concealed by countersinking and covering the head with solder.

Mounting Controls on Truck. Some builders prefer to have the reversing switch mounted directly to the truck. Thus we obtain an integral unit which can be wired without resorting to jumpers which must be disconnected when the motor is removed for servicing. In many of the smaller cars this is impractical. Of course where DC is used with permag motors, no reversing switch is needed. In figure 71 is shown a method of attaching a rectifier directly to the motor (K and D) and a bracket for holding a drum type reverse switch. The switch must be reduced in width by at least 1/8" in order to get it in the available space.

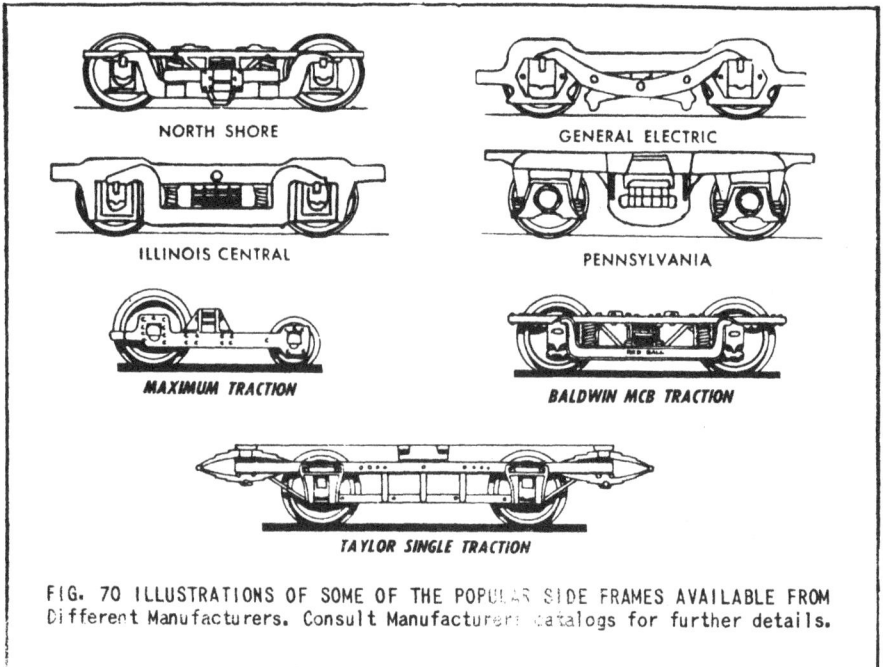

NORTH SHORE

GENERAL ELECTRIC

ILLINOIS CENTRAL

PENNSYLVANIA

MAXIMUM TRACTION

BALDWIN MCB TRACTION

TAYLOR SINGLE TRACTION

FIG. 70 ILLUSTRATIONS OF SOME OF THE POPULAR SIDE FRAMES AVAILABLE FROM Different Manufacturers. Consult Manufacturers catalogs for further details.

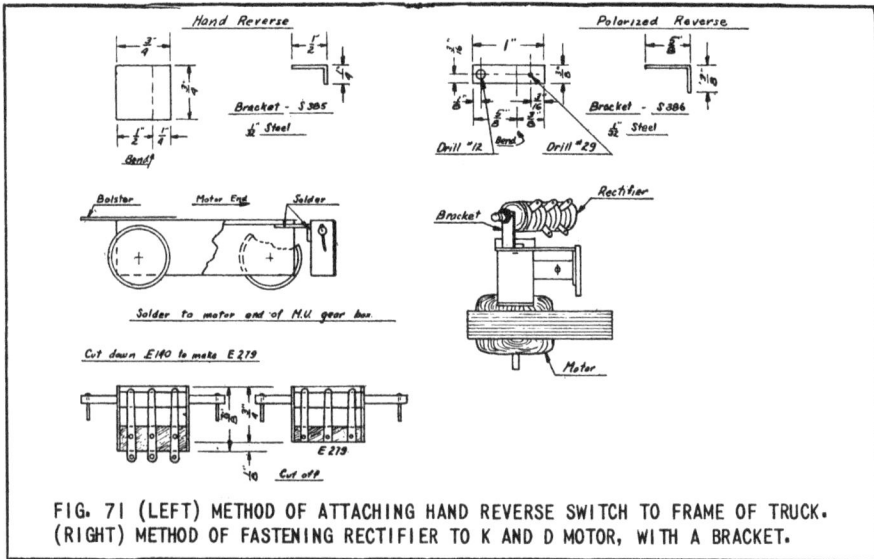

FIG. 71 (LEFT) METHOD OF ATTACHING HAND REVERSE SWITCH TO FRAME OF TRUCK. (RIGHT) METHOD OF FASTENING RECTIFIER TO K AND D MOTOR, WITH A BRACKET.

For three rail operation the outside collector shoe should be attached directly to the truck so it will follow the wheels at all times. A bracket for mounting this is shown in figure 72. For a center third rail, the pick-up may be mounted in a similar manner or to an insulated block attached to the bottom of the gear box between the wheels. The placing of these extra parts often creates a problem. With exclusive overhead pick-up, or two rail we do not have this trouble.

Overhead Trolley Poles and Pantagraphs. The mounting of trolley poles and pantagraphs offer no particular problem. Some trolley builders like to be able to remove these appurtenances when not required. Trolley poles are made to screw into bushings which in turn are screwed or otherwise mounted to the car roof. Pantagraphs can be provided with dress snaps (representing the supporting insulators) and the mating half of the snap applied to the pantagraph platform. This provides a

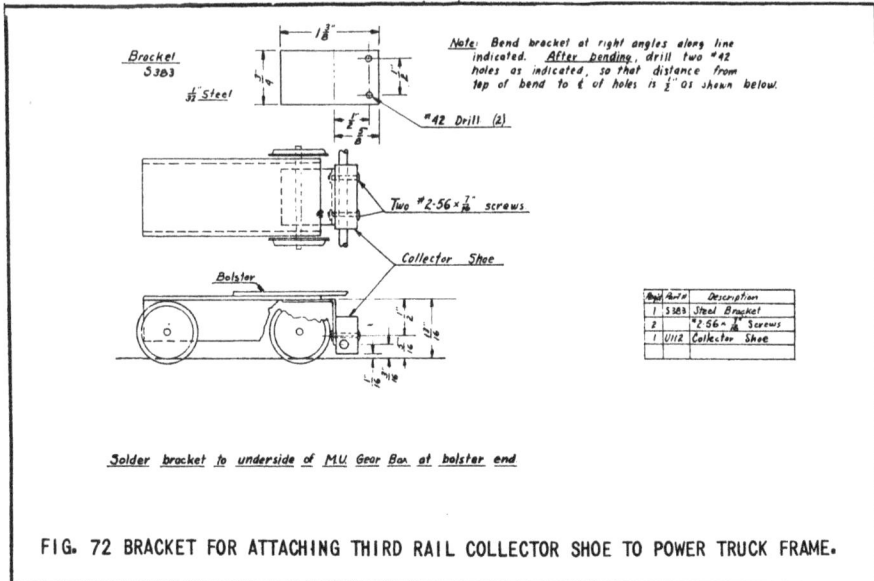

FIG. 72 BRACKET FOR ATTACHING THIRD RAIL COLLECTOR SHOE TO POWER TRUCK FRAME.

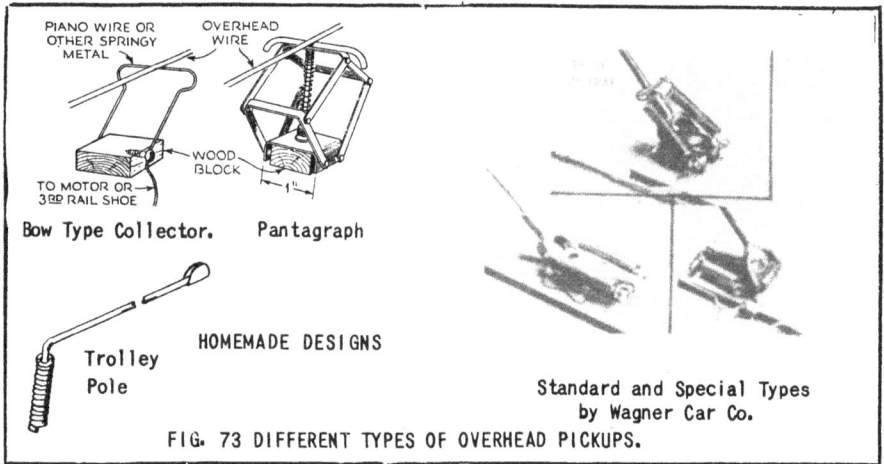

FIG. 73 DIFFERENT TYPES OF OVERHEAD PICKUPS.

simple method of taking on and off the "pants".

For those who do not like the pantagraph pick-up and have trouble with a trolley we suggest the type of overhead collector known to our English cousins as a "collector bow". I do not recall any trolley system in the United States that uses this arrangement, but regardless of prototype authenticity it offers an excellent overhead pick-up that can be used with a single trolley wire or catenary. Figure 73 illustrates a style of this type.

If trolley hooks are used for holding the trolley while down, and if these hooks are used in connection with a reversing circuit as described in the electrical chapter, it is suggested that they be provided with a small spring which will hold the trolley pole rigid. This will prevent the pole from jiggling under the hook which in turn causes the circuit to be interrupted resulting in jerky running. See figure 74.

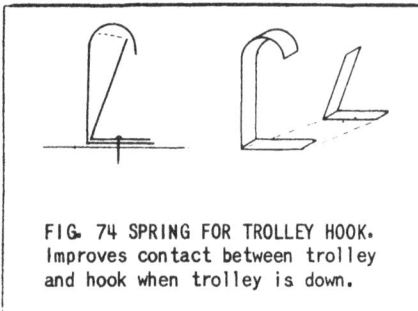

FIG. 74 SPRING FOR TROLLEY HOOK. Improves contact between trolley and hook when trolley is down.

Connecting Two Motors Together. When more than one motor is used on a car the several motors should be connected in multiple. This means that all the ground connections come to one ground terminal and all the pick-up connections are connected to the pick-up, whatever it is, (trolley, third-rail shoes or truck). With permag motors this is not much of a problem because there are only two connections but with a series motor there are four wires for each motor and it might be questioned just how these wires are interconnected. If you will consider that you have only one motor and connect that up so it runs in the correct way, then connect the other motor so it runs in the same direction and connect that to the same terminals as you did the first motor.

If you are installing reversing mechanisms on the car the problem gets a little more complicated. If you wish to use one switch for two motors, you must connect the two fields in parallel and the two armatures in parallel, then consider the fields as one and the armature as one as far as the reverse switch connections are concerned. Be sure, when you connect the fields in parallel, that both are connected so they will produce rotation in the same direction. In case you find one motor runs in one direction while the other runs opposite, just interchange the connections for one of the fields (reverse wires).

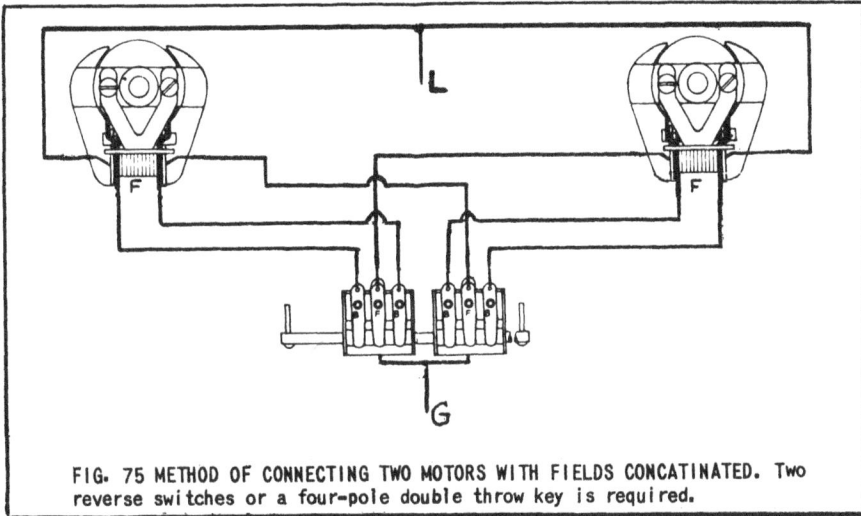

FIG. 75 METHOD OF CONNECTING TWO MOTORS WITH FIELDS CONCATINATED. Two reverse switches or a four-pole double throw key is required.

With more than one motor in the same car it frequently happens that one motor takes over more of the load than the other so one motor either drags or spins. In actual railroad practice this is overcome by cross connecting the field of one motor to the armature of the other. This will cause the loading of one motor to adjust the speed of the other to the balancing point. This is called concatination. It can be resorted to in model practice with good results but calls for careful wiring. This only applies to series motors.

Jumpers between Cars. When several cars are operated together as a train it is desirable to interconnect the cars so that trolleys on the trailer units will be connected in parallel with the trolley on the power car. To carry the circuit between the cars a jumper wire should be installed either to simulate the usual inter-car wires (above the end doors) or the air hose. In either case a disconnect type of connector should be used in this jumper wire so the circuit can be broken when the cars are uncoupled.

Headlights and Car Lights. Operating lights always add to the realism. You can install a headlight, at each end of the car and connect these as shown in diagram 76 so that the forward light will be lit and the rear light dim regardless which direction you are running. In other words, the reversing of the lights will follow the reversing of the motor. With this scheme the rear light is never out, but just dim. Or, if you prefer, you can install a separate switch for the headlights so either can be connected or the train operated without lights.

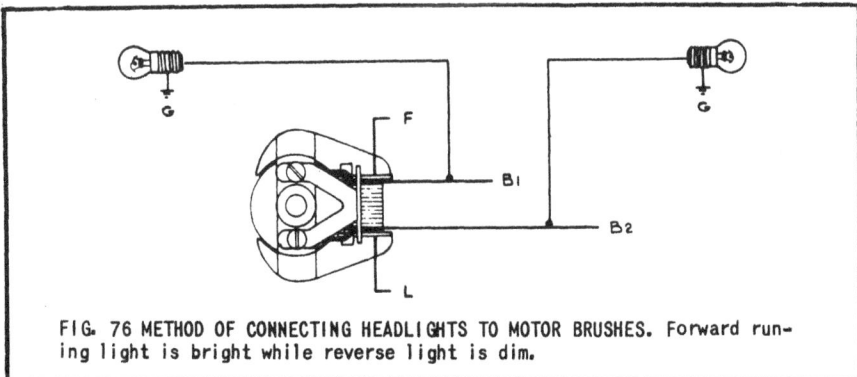

FIG. 76 METHOD OF CONNECTING HEADLIGHTS TO MOTOR BRUSHES. Forward running light is bright while reverse light is dim.

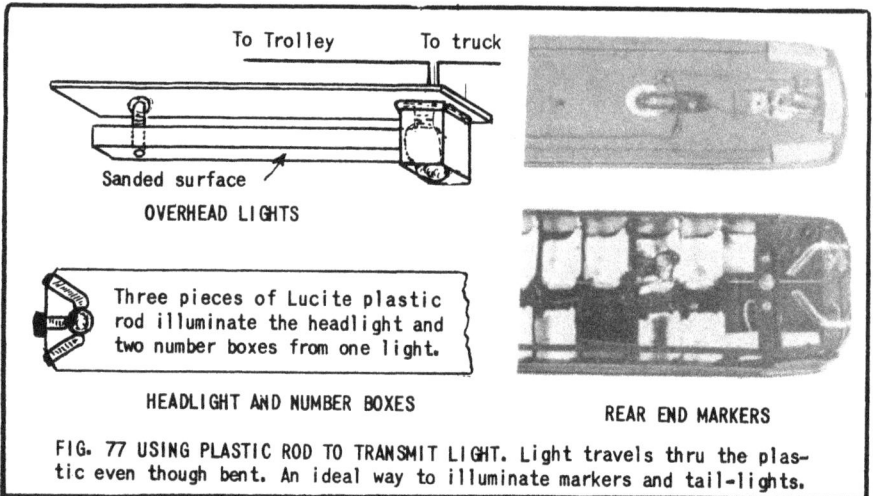

To Trolley   To truck

Sanded surface

OVERHEAD LIGHTS

Three pieces of Lucite plastic
rod illuminate the headlight and
two number boxes from one light.

HEADLIGHT AND NUMBER BOXES

REAR END MARKERS

FIG. 77 USING PLASTIC ROD TO TRANSMIT LIGHT. Light travels thru the plastic even though bent. An ideal way to illuminate markers and tail-lights.

Interior lights mounted in the roof of the car are also realistic. The motormans compartment can be blocked out so it will be dark. For the observation car a tail sign makes a nice show piece. Markers, on the rear car may be illuminated by running lucite tubing from an interior light to colored lenses carried at the marker locations.

If 12 volt lights are used for this lighting, connect them all in parallel and to the ground and pick-up connections so all the lights will be in multiple with the motor. If smaller voltage lights are used then connect them in series groups so the voltage of each string equals 12 (two 6 volt lamps or five 2-1/2 volt lamps). If you cannot work out a series connection then place a suitable resistor in series with the lamp to reduce the voltage to the proper level. In determining the amount of resistance figure 4 ohms for each volt of "loss" you need. In other words a 24 ohms resistor in series with a six volt lamp is right for 12 volts.

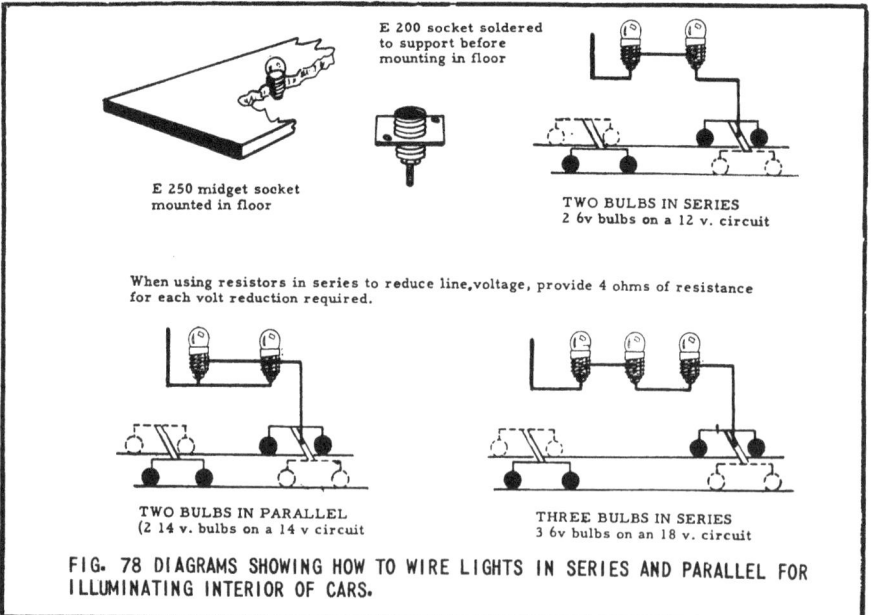

E 200 socket soldered
to support before
mounting in floor

E 250 midget socket
mounted in floor

TWO BULBS IN SERIES
2 6v bulbs on a 12 v. circuit

When using resistors in series to reduce line voltage, provide 4 ohms of resistance
for each volt reduction required.

TWO BULBS IN PARALLEL
(2 14 v. bulbs on a 14 v circuit

THREE BULBS IN SERIES
3 6v bulbs on an 18 v. circuit

FIG. 78 DIAGRAMS SHOWING HOW TO WIRE LIGHTS IN SERIES AND PARALLEL FOR ILLUMINATING INTERIOR OF CARS.

Chapter 7

BUILDING A TROLLEY CAR

In the last section we described motors and transmission devices and in this we turn to a general description of the construction of the car body itself. Perhaps this section should have preceded the one before but to the writer it seemed more logical to develop the material in this Guide from the track to the car. In as much as each section is a unit, the reader may follow any reading sequence he desires. I must also ask the readers indulgence in presenting the subject matter of this section based on the designs and methods with which I am most familiar. While other manufacturers offer excellent parts and kits and each has his own style of construction, the basic construction methods are sufficiently similar that what is said here will prove helpful with most any line of parts or kits.

The Car Body. This consists of the roof, floor, sides and ends. The roof and floor are usually of wood, the sides may be paper, wood, metal or plastic. The ends may be wood or die-cast metal or made of paper or plastic as part of the side. In another type of construction all parts of the car body are individual castings, may be cast in two halves or the entire body may be an integral casting. Much depends on the scale, type of car being modeled and the degree of detail to be incorporated.

In general the most suitable material and construction method is used that will carry the prototype construction into the model. Again, the model builder who achieves an exhibition model may go to extremes in duplicating every construction feature as well as detail. For the most of us a model that is easy to build but realistic in appearance, is a good enough goal.

The roof, when made of wood, is cut to length from a section that has been made as a moulding on a wood working machine called a "sticker". Roof sections, of this type follow the contours of the clerestory, (Monitor) arch and streamlined designs. The ends are shaped to round off and complete the contour. The underside of the roof is recessed to receive the sides and the ends of the roof must be recessed if die-cast ends are used. The floor is cut to conform to the roof dimensions. It must also have an opening at one end if the concealed type of motor unit is to be installed, but not if the under-floor type will be used. In the all cast car body the floor may be omitted.

Die-cast ends come complete with window, door, rivet and scribing detail formed in the castings. Such castings also have lugs on their inner side for attaching roof and

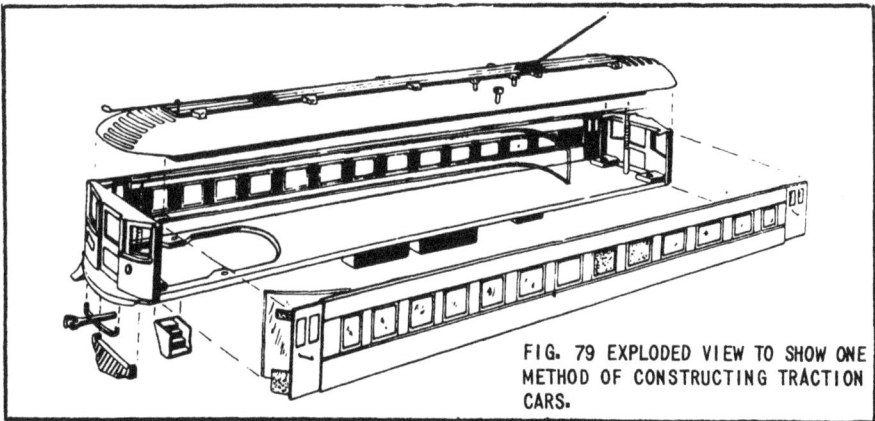

FIG. 79 EXPLODED VIEW TO SHOW ONE METHOD OF CONSTRUCTING TRACTION CARS.

(Above, left) Start of the car body. Floor, part of sides and end in place. Note hole in floor for power truck suspension.

(Above, right) More of the sides and ends in place. Note the openings in the floor for stair wells.

(Left) Verticle pieces added to sides and ends to form window openings. Cross-supports added also trolley reel and anti-climber to front. Trucks are shown in place.

(Below, left) Complete car shown with roof detached. Lights for interior wiring in place. Car has been painted.

(Below, right) Finished Car lettered ready for its first run.
(Photos courtesy R. M. Wagner)

FIG. 80 STEP BY STEP ILLUSTRATIONS TO SHOW METHOD OF BUILDING A TRACTION CAR FROM SCRATCH.

floor sections and their surface may have cored holes for locating grab-irons and other superimposed detail parts. Wood ends are cut from moulded sections but come without windows or doors or details. These the builder incorporates. When the ends are part of the sides (paper, metal or plastic) an end may be a part of each side or half an end may be included at the end of each side. In one case the joints between side pieces will come at the opposite corners of the car body and in the other at the center of each end. Ends are usually labeled according to their door and window arrangements as "two window and door", or "three window" end.

The kind of end construction varies with types of cars and frequently the model builder is unable to find a stock end to meet his specifications. In this event he has the choice of building up an end from scratch or modifying the closest approach to his design. This may mean enlarging or shrinking windows, changing the door size or even disecting the end and rebuilding it completely. This is not too difficult to do but calls on the builders ingenuity as well as skill. The writer has seen examples of such modifications that were excellent reproductions yet were done very simply with the aid of cement and solder, and everyday tools.

The material used for the sides should follow the prototype. Thus metal sides with embossed rivets for metal car bodies and wood sides with scribed lines for the older wooden car bodies. With plastic either construction can be copied but with cardboard it is not as easy to represent either scoring or rivets without distorting the side mater-

ial. However some excellent sides have been built from cardboard of the poster-board variety which can be readily scribed and with rivets overlayed in the form of strips, which are cemented on.

Manufacturers supply sides with window and door openings stamped out, panels (for window frames) formed and rivets rolled in. This applies particularly to metal and cardboard sides. Wood sides with scribed board lines are available but are not generally complete with window openings cut out. One manufacturer (^{0}) can supply wood sides with openings cut representing the old style window that has the arched top with stained glass upper sash. No doubt other designs will be added as trolley model building becomes more popular.

The car body is constructed by first attaching the ends to the roof and floor and then the sides. When sides are panelled and are to have windows (cellutate-acetate) it is necessary to include cardboard spacers between the sides and window material to offset the panels. Usually the spacers and cellutate is fastened to the sides before the sides are attached to the roof and floor and end framework. With the latest type of adhesive (Goo^0) it is possible to cement most any material to any other material. Thus wood, metal or cardboard sides are cemented to the car frame rather than nailing. With this type of adhesive a certain time is required for obtaining a strong bond and it helps if the various parts are held together with rubber bands or string for a few hours.

Some prefer to complete the roof and underbody details before adding the sides. If the roof is to be made removable it cannot be attached to the

FIG. 81 PACIFIC ELECTRIC SIDE DOOR TROLLEY CAR. See page 67 for drawing.

FIG. 82 SEMI-CONVERTABLE TROLLEY.
See page 62 for Drawings.

FIG. 83 DOUBLE TRUCK SAFETY CAR.
See page 64 for Drawings.

sides. In this case cross pieces should be added to hold the sides at several locations, or a small channel attached to the upper edge of the sides to stiffen the side and serve as a support on which to rest the roof. Each builder has his own method of making the roof removable and the construction followed will depend on the side material being used and the end construction.

Underbody Detailing. To complete the underbody of a car we start out with a centersill (underframe) with body bolsters (for supporting the trucks) and two or more crossbearers. The power car will require a special mounting bracket for the power truck but the trailing truck will mount on the body bolster. In the case of trailing cars, without power, both trucks will be mounted on the body bolsters.

A car with vestibules, or open platforms will have a platform step for each side door. Strap steps are used under the motorman's and baggage doors. Other underbody details include a wide variety of equipment such as resistor boxes, battery boxes, tanks for air and water, brake cylinders, triple valve, generator, and sometimes steam traps. No two cars are alike in their underbody

parts and if the builder wishes to be correct to prototype he must be willing to do a little research work in inspecting his type of car or securing photographs from the railroad company or builder. Getting information from the railroads and builders is difficult today because requests coming from so many model builders have to be ignored.

Roof Detailing. The detailing of the roof includes the ventilators which are typed by roof style. Globe Vents, are used over washrooms and by some roads for general ventilation. The garland or monitor type is used with the clerestory roof and the Utility style with arch roofs. The number of vents varies with the type of car and the type of ventilation scheme. With the latest air conditioning equipment there are fewer vents on the roof.

The roof may have a roof walk, special platforms for mounting the pantagraph (if used), drip strips over the doors, grab-irons or hand-holds and perhaps an aerial for radio reception. Trolley pole mounts and hooks are used where needed. The roof walk is similar to that used on freight car roofs. Drip strips over doors are made from small pieces of square wire. Grabs are made from

FIG. 84 FREIGHT MOTOR CAR.
See page 66 for Drawings

staples. Small ceramic beads are used for insulators. Straightened pieces of round wire attached to the heads of nails or screws holding the insulators make the aerial.

The roof may also carry the headlight or an indication sign holder. If no stock parts are available for these special details the builder must resort to his own ingenuity in constructing them.

Other Detailing. Vertical hand-holds are placed at each side of vestibule doors and at least on one side of baggage and postal doors. Holes are drilled in the ends and pierced in the sides to receive these. They are cemented or soldered in place. There are at least two grab-irons on each end of cars. Sometimes additional grab-irons are placed on the ends of cars to serve as a ladder to reach the roof.

Nearly all trolley cars and many interurbans carry pilots at the front end. These may take the form of a basket, be in the form of grids or similar to locomotive pilots. For some styles die-cast models are available while others must be painstakingly made by soldering together many small pieces of wire. This work can be made easier by setting up a simple jig to hold the parts while being joined. A well made pilot adds a great deal to the appearance of the car.

Diaphragms are not a usual part of cars when operated in trains, but chains are hung from car to car as protection to passengers who wish to transfer between cars. Chains are also hung across the front and rear doors.

The coupler is so hung on trolley cars that it can swing almost the full width of the car body. This is necessary to enable the cars to navigate sharp turns. On interurban cars the coupler mountings is similar to standard passenger cars.

The interior of cars can be fitted out with seats, wash bowls and toilets, tables and chairs. Carpets made from "flocked" paper are available in several colors. Miniature figures, in seated position, add further realism. Interior details and lights should be installed before the sides are put on, or the roof should be made movable so that the interior can be worked on at any time.

Painting and Lettering. While this is mentioned last it does not necessarily mean that the painting should be left to the last. Some prefer to paint the parts before applying them to the car body. The inside of the car should be painted before the sides or roof is attached.

When the body is completed, sand the roof carefully and seal with Plastico Rok or Sanding Sealer and paint black, or whatever color is called for. The roof should receive this treatment before the details are added and then finish painted after everything is in place. Windows should be covered with masking tape when painting the sides so as not to cover them with paint streaks. Allow the paint to dry hard before applying lettering decals.

Decals are also available for simulating the frosted glass of washroom windows, venetian blinds and the special arched glass clerestory windows. Where striping is required, this can be put on too with decals. Stripe decals are available in many colors and widths.

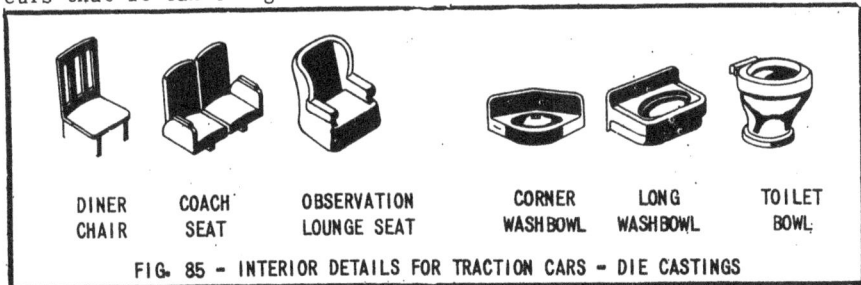

| DINER CHAIR | COACH SEAT | OBSERVATION LOUNGE SEAT | CORNER WASHBOWL | LONG WASHBOWL | TOILET BOWL |

FIG. 85 - INTERIOR DETAILS FOR TRACTION CARS - DIE CASTINGS

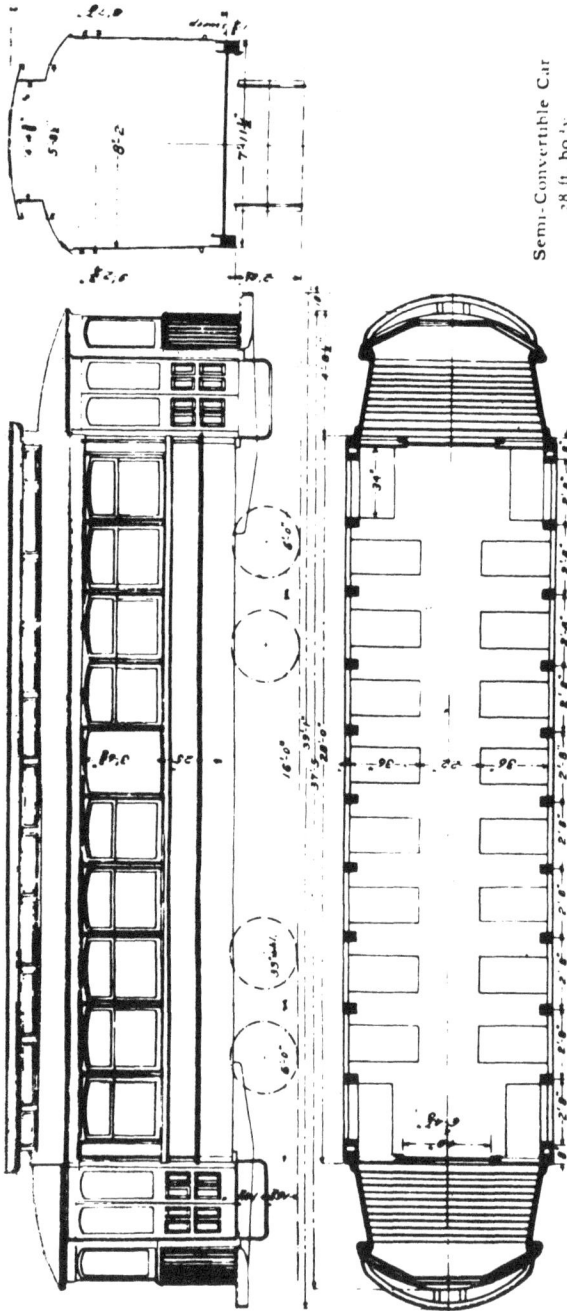

Semi-Convertible Car
28 ft. body
J. G. Brill Company

FIG. 86 PLANS FOR SEMI-CONVERTABLE TROLLEY CAR, built by J. G. Brill Co. See page 60 (Fig. 82) for Illustration.

BUILDING A TROLLEY CAR

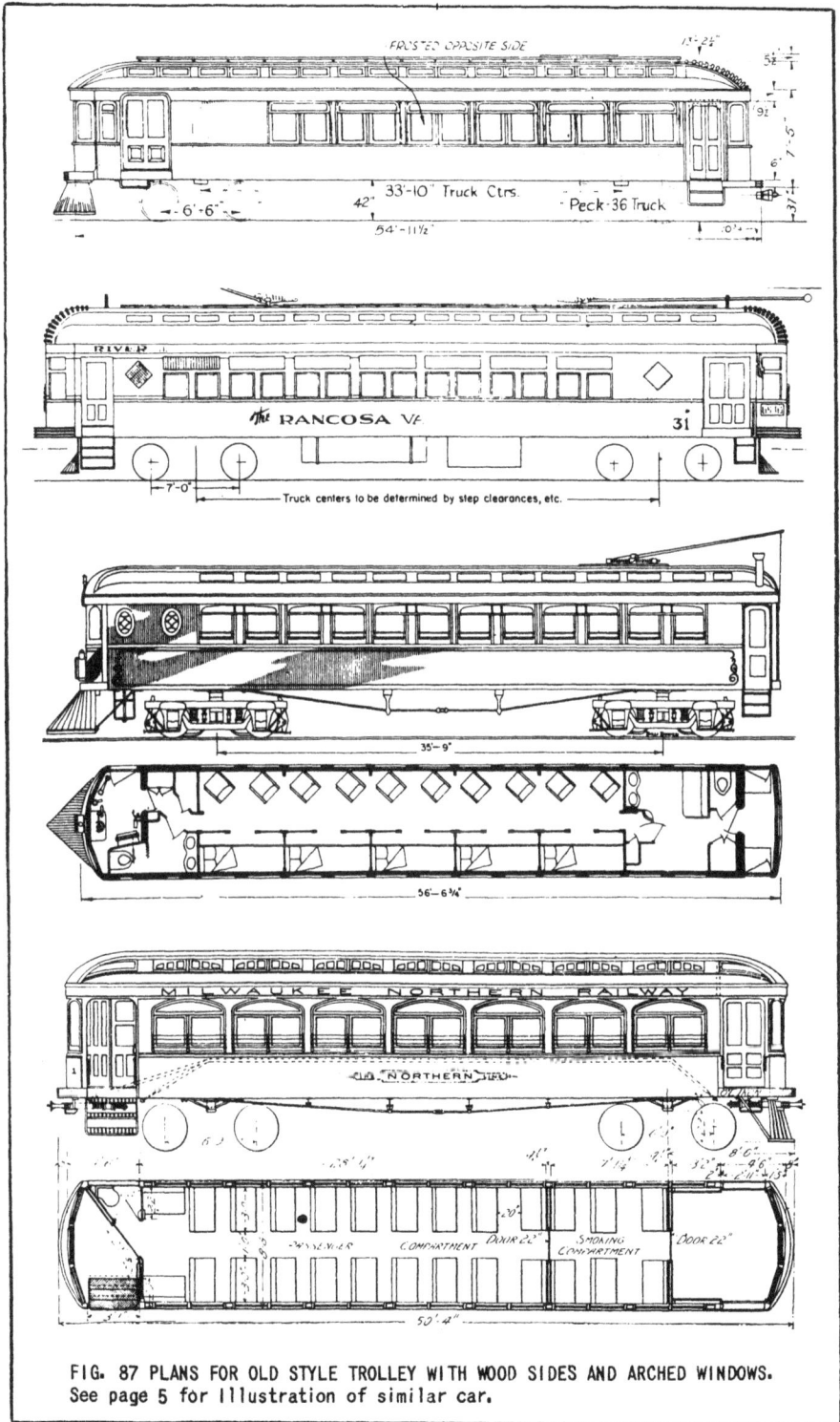

FIG. 87 PLANS FOR OLD STYLE TROLLEY WITH WOOD SIDES AND ARCHED WINDOWS. See page 5 for Illustration of similar car.

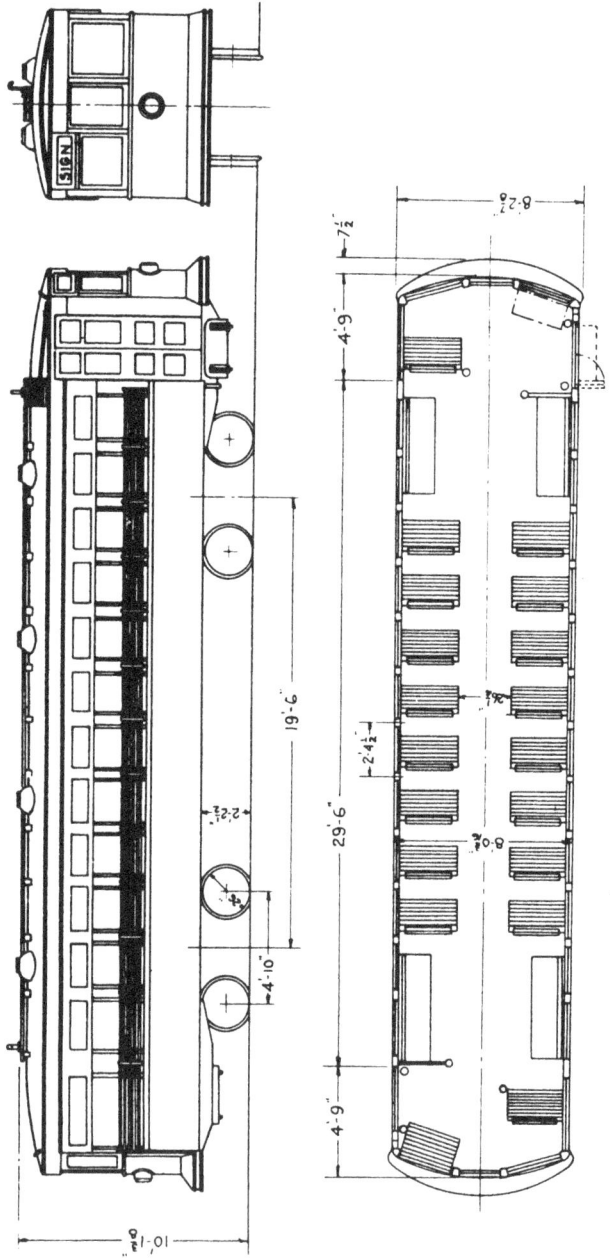

FIG. 88 STANDARD DOUBLE TRUCK SAFETY CAR. Built by the J. G. Brill Co.
See page 60 (Fig. 83) for Illustration of this car.

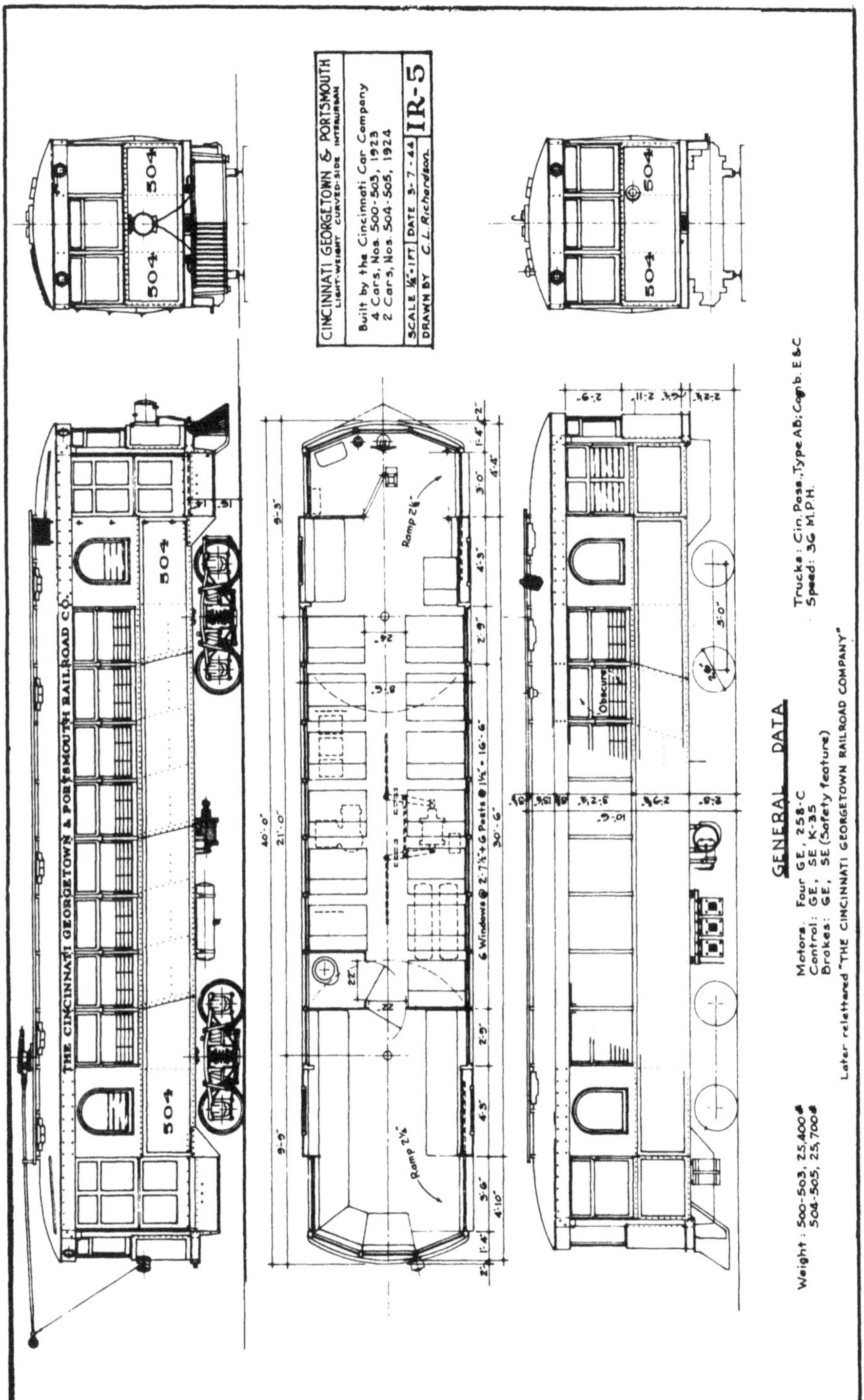

FIG. 89 LIGHT WEIGHT CURVED SIDE INTERURBAN. Built by Cincinnati Car Co.
See page 6 for Illustration of this car.

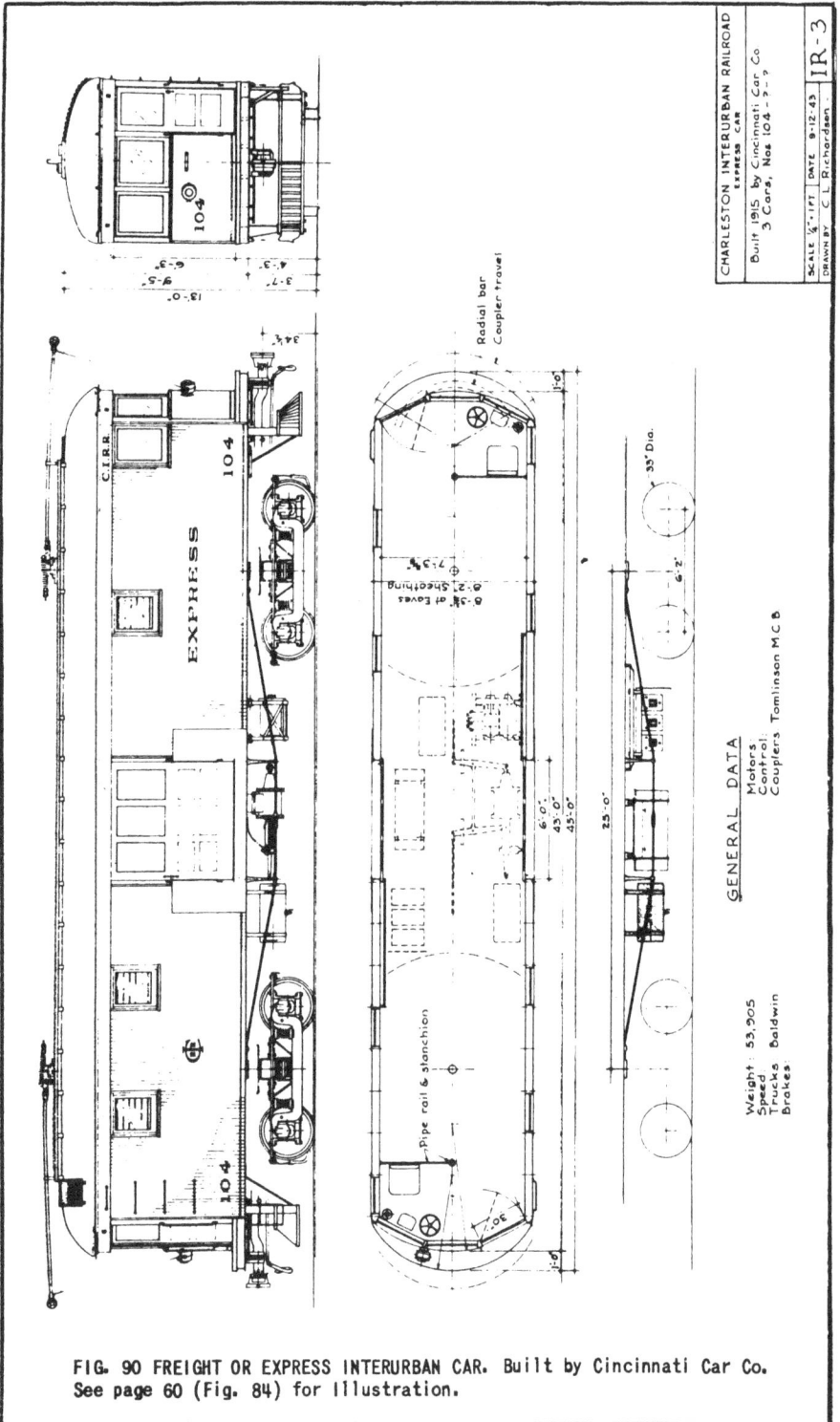

FIG. 90 FREIGHT OR EXPRESS INTERURBAN CAR. Built by Cincinnati Car Co.
See page 60 (Fig. 84) for Illustration.

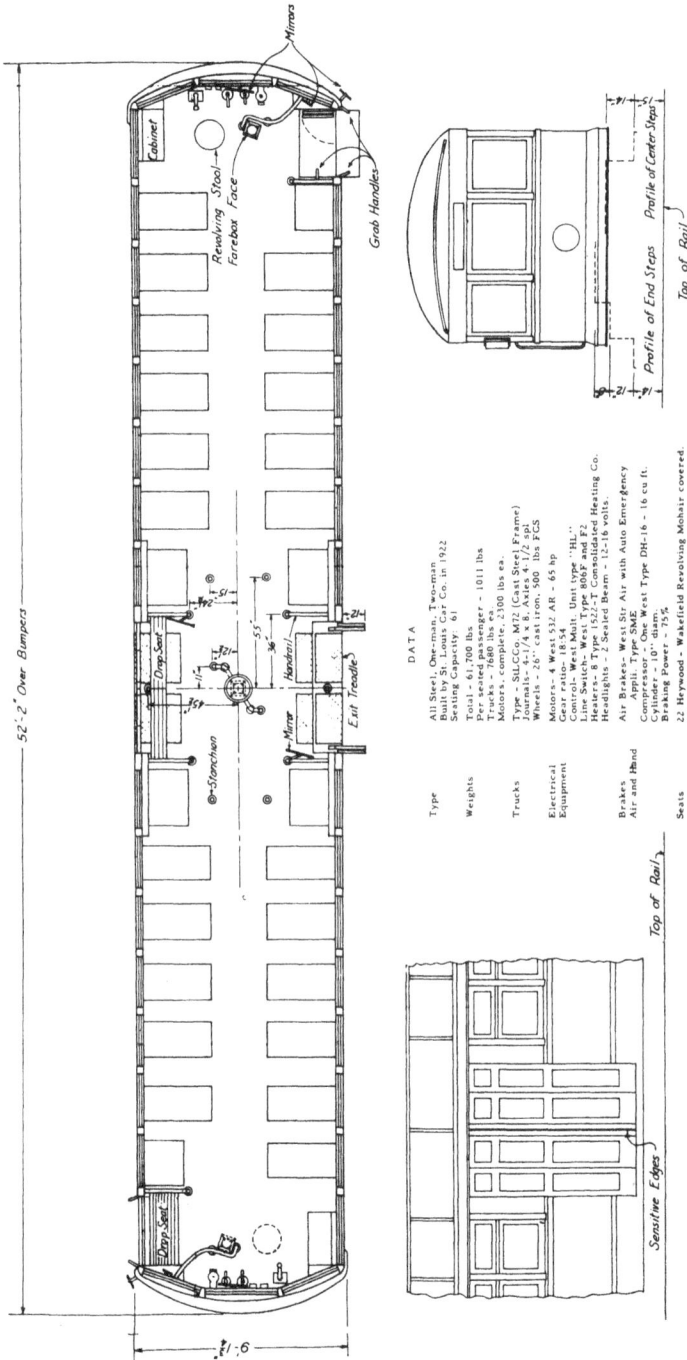

DATA

Type	All Steel, One-man, Two-man Built by St. Louis Car Co. in 1922 Seating Capacity: 61
Weights	Total - 61,700 lbs. Per seated passenger - 1011 lbs Trucks - 7680 lbs ea. Motors - complete, 2100 lbs ea.
Trucks	Type - StLCCo. M72 (Cast Steel Frame) Journals- 4-1/4 x 8, Axles 4-1/2 spl Wheels - 26" cast iron, 500 lbs FCS
Electrical Equipment	Motors- 4 West 532 AR - 65 hp Gear ratio- 18:54 Control- West Mult. Unit type "HL" Line Switch- West Type 806F and F2 Heaters- 8 Type 162-T Consolidated Heating Co. Headlights 2 Sealed Beam - 12-16 volts.
Brakes Air and Hand	Air Brakes - West Str Air with Auto Emergency Appli. Type SME Compressor - One West Type DH-16 - 16 cu ft. Cylinder - 10" diam. Braking Power - 75%
Seats	22 Heywood - Wakefield Revolving Mohair covered. 6 Longitudinal - Mohair covered. 4 folding wood

Applies to 600 and 700 PE cars.

FIG. 91 SIDE DOOR, ONE-MAN OPERATION TROLLEY CAR.
See Fig. 81 for Illustration.

Chapter 8

BIBLIOGRAPHY TO TROLLEY ARTICLES

The following abbreviations are used to identify articles listed:
MB   MODEL BUILDER, published by The Lionel Corp. 15 East 26th
St., N.Y.C. (Now out of print)
MC   MODEL CRAFTSMAN, (now called "Railroad Model Craftsman
and includes The Modelmaker and Miniature Railroading)
published by Model Craftsman Publishing Co., Ramsey, N.J.
MN   MINIATURE RAILROADING - see above
MR   MODEL RAILROADER, published by Kalmbach Publishing Co.,
1027 N. 7th St., Milwaukee, Wis.
MD   MODEL RAILROAD DIGEST, published by Louis Hertz, 4 Colvin
Road, Scarsdale N.Y. (Publication discontinued).
The figures in the second column indicate the month and year.
The figure in the third column indicates the page.

Other magazines, not included in this bibliography but which
print information on traction or trolleys of interest to model
builders are listed below:
HO MONTHLY, Published by The HO Monthly Publishing Co.,
865 Belmont Ave., Philadelphia, Pa.
THE WHISTLE STOP - P.O. Box 1951 Cincinnati, Ohio.
RAILWAY AGE, published by Simmonds-Boardman Pub. Co.,
30 Church St., New York City.
RAILROAD MAGAZINE, published by Popular Publications, Inc.
205 East 42nd St., New York City

BIBLIOGRAPHY TO TROLLEY ARTICLES

|---|---|---|---|
Eastern Ohio Cars	MC	11-48	36
Electric-			
-Trolley Locomotive	MC	11-48	30
-Trolley Locomotive	MC	12-48	10
-Trolley Locomotive	MC	1-49	12
Electrified Railroads	MC	1-46	28
Elevated-			
-Railway	MC	12-42	10
-Railway	MC	1-43	10
-Railway	MC	6-45	20
Enclosed Motor Drive	MC	10-48	22
Flat Cars	MC	2-43	10
Flat Head Wood Screws			
for 3rd Rail	MR	7-41	355
Four-Hook Reverse	MR	3-44	129
Four-Wheel City Car	MD	4-40	14
Frogs, Location	MR	1-49	16
Frogs, Section Insula-			
tors, Suspension	MC	4-40	25
"Gay Nineties" Street Car	MC	12-39	12
Governor Corbett, Steam			
Dummy	MC	7-48	24
How to Draw Plans for			
Interurbans	MC	12-44	18
ICC Trolley, 0 ga.	MR	5-49	33
IC Suburban Coach	MR	4-43	182
IC Suburban Trailer	MC	9-45	8
Ice Trolley & Line Car	MC	8-48	12
Indiana RR Coach and			
Baggage	MC	10-40	13
Indiana RR Combine	MR	7-43	304
Indiana RR Parlor and			
Coach	MC	10-40	13
Indianapolis Railway			
Street Car	MR	1-48	38
Insulators	MR	2-38	85
Interesting Terminal			
Operation	MC	10-47	24
Interstate-			
-Lines	MR	4-38	149
-Public Service Cars	MC	6-42	30
-Public Service Parlor-			
Diner	MC	6-43	13
Interurban-			
-and Trolley Kinks	MR	10-40	543
-Car	MR	4-46	252
-Car, Old-Time	MR	3-44	130
-Car, Open	MC	11-41	14
-Car Plans	MR	10-41	517
-Car, Rebuilt	MC	2-42	24
-Depot and Substation	MC	2-45	15
-Diner	MC	3-47	28
-Freight Cars	MC	3-42	30
-Freight Cars	MC	4-42	30
-Layout	MR	5-40	275
-Layout, Large	MC	6-46	18
-Layout, Loops & Branch	MC	4-40	25
-Line	MD	6-40	4
-Lines	MR	4-38	199
-Lines in Restricted			
Space	MR	7-42	325
-Lines, Modeling	MR	1-46	36
-Official Car	MC	3-49	8
Interurban			
-Official Car	MC	4-49	20
-Official Car	MC	5-49	16
-Power Truck	MR	10-40	533
-Sand Car	MC	9-47	8
-Sleeper	MR	5-44	217
-Spotlight	MR	2-49	57
-3/8" Narrow Gauge	MR	4-38	149
-Windows	MR	1-4	51
Interurbans-			
-in Restricted Areas	MR	7-40	398
-in Restricted Areas	MR	7-42	325
Iowa Interurban	MR	12-47	996
Japanese Street Car	MC	4-48	50
Jewett Car	MD	5-40	8
Keeping Trolley on Wire	MC	10-40	24
Key System Articulated			
Cars	MC	9-47	26
Lake Shore Electric	MR	5-49	33
Lake Shore Electric,			
Coach Smoker	MC	3-40	15
Lake Erie & Southern	MR	11-49	36
LaNal Model	MC	11-38	14
Large City Car	MC	6-47	29
Layout Doctor-			
-Trolley with Steam	MC	10-48	7
-Trolley with Steam	MC	11-48	14
-Trolley with Steam	MC	12-48	30
-Trolley with Steam	MC	3-49	16
-Trolley with Steam	MC	4-49	9
-Trolley with Steam	MC	5-49	28
-Trolley with Steam	MC	6-49	23
Layouts Depend on Space	MC	1-42	8
Lehigh Valley Super-			
Detailed Model	MD	4-40	19
Liberty Belle Limited	MC	5-41	40
Liberty Belle Limited	MC	6-41	32
Mail, Passenger, Baggage			
Car	MC	4-45	14
Making Pantographs	MR	5-45	14
Melbourne Tram	MC	9-45	19
Memoirs of a Model			
Railroader	MC	2-48	14
Memoirs of a Model			
Railroader	MC	3-48	10
Michigan RR, Coach-			
Smoker-Baggage	MC	6-43	13
Milwaukee Northern	MR	3-49	40
Miniature Models	MN	7-40	4
Model Traction Layout	MC	11-47	16
Model Trolley Line	MC	8-47	28
Modern-Car Models	MC	4-38	20
Montreal & Southern			
Counties	MD	10-40	11
Mounting Pantographs	MR	5-39	247
MU Drive	MR	7-38	284
North Shore, Coach with			
Smoker	MC	8-40	24
North Shore Freight Motor	MR	6-40	344
North Shore Wood Coach	MR	2-41	81
Observation Car	MC	5-43	13
Operating Trolleys	MR	10-40	535
Outdoor Interurban	MR	11-39	553

69

TERMS COMMONLY USED
IN THE ELECTRIC TRACTION FIELD

ANTI-CLIMBER: A corrugated channel section used in place of bumper to prevent cars in collision from over-riding.

ARCH-BAR: The top member of a diamond-shaped trussed side frame of a truck.

ARCHED ROOF: A roof of a continuous symmetrical curve from one side of car to the other.

BARBER CAR: A single truck car for city service, with square ends and arch roof.

BELT RAIL: A narrow strip of wood framed horizontally into the side posts of a car body, below the windows on outside.

BODY BOLSTER: A cross member of the body underframing of a double truck car which transmits the load carried by the longitudinal sills to the center plate.

BOW COLLECTOR: A flexible horizontal bar or light roller which slides on the underside of an overhead trolley wire-used instead of a trolley wheel.

BRAKE CYLINDER: An iron cylinder bolted to the underframe of a car and containing a piston which is forced outwardly by the admission of compressed air. This motion is transmitted by mechanical link-to the brake beam which applies pressure through the brake shoes to the wheels.

BRAKE HOSE: A laminated rubber and cotton tubing. It forms a flexible connection between the brake pipes of two adjoining cars, through which compressed air for operating the train brakes is conducted.

BRAKE SHOE: A curved block of metal, which is pressed against the tread of a car wheel when the brakes are applied.

BULKHEAD: A cross partition in car body.

CALIFORNIA TYPE CAR: A car designed for all year service. The body is built with a closed compartment in the center, and with cross bench open seats occupying the remaining space between platforms.

CANOPY: A term applied to a platform roof.

CAR BODY: The main structure of a car which is mounted on one or two trucks.

CARLINE: One of the transverse members of the roof framing of a car on which the roof boards are laid.

CENTER PIN: A round steel bolt passing through the body and truck center on which the truck swivels. (King pin.)

CENTER SIDE ENTRANCE CAR: A car built with an entrance door in the center of the side of the car body.

CENTER SILLS: The central pair of longitudinal members of car body underframe.

CLERESTORY: An obsolete name for the deck of a monitor car type roof.

COMBINATION CAR: Any car having one or more compartments for passengers and a separate compartment for baggage or mail.

CONTROLLER: The complete assemblage of parts whereby the switching necessary to regulate the speed and direction of rotation of the motors is accomplished.

CONVERTABLE CAR: A type of car which can be operated with the side entirely enclosed with panels and with window sashes, or with both panels and the sashes removed, leaving the space between posts entirely open from floor to plate.

COUPLER: The iron bar and head by means of which two cars are connected for train operation.

DASHER: The curved metal plate or wooden panels enclosing the end of an electric car platform.

DECK: The upper part of a monitor roof.

DESTINATION SIGN: A printed sign or marker on a car to indicate its route.

DOUBLE DECK CAR: A car with seats on the roof as well as within the body.

DOUBLE END CAR: A car with similar platforms and equipment on each end and which may be operated in either direction.

DOUBLE TROLLEY SYSTEM: A system of current distribution employing two trolley wires, eliminating the rail as a return circuit.

DRAFT GEAR: A general term embracing all of the appliances and attachments by which one car is made to pull another.

DRAWBAR: An iron bar or casting with a socket head for receiving a coupling link by which two cars are coupled together.

DRIP RAIL: A narrow moulding above the side windows, on the outside, to prevent water from running down on the windows.

EAVES: The lowest edge of a car roof.

EAVES MOLDING: A molding to cover the overlapping edge of the roofing canvas.

EMPIRE DECK: A roof for interurban cars.

FENDER: A projecting basket attached to the front of a street car to catch persons when struck.

FLAG: Red, white or green cloth displayed on rear or front as a marker or signal.

FLAG HOLDER: A socket for holding a flag.

GRAB HANDLE: A verticle handle secured to the body or platform corner post above the platform steps.

HEADLIGHT: A lamp and reflector mounted on the dasher or on top of front platform hood to light up the track ahead.

JOURNAL BOX: The bearing in which the axle of the truck rotates.

LETTER BOARD: A board on the outside of a car just below the eaves.

71

LINE CAR: A work car for repairing the overhead structures and wires.

MARKER LAMP: A signal lamp mounted on the corner posts of a car to indicate its class and direction of movement.

MAXIMUM TRACTION TRUCK: A single motor truck in which more weight is carried on the driving axle than on the pony axle.

M. C. B. TYPE TRUCK: One designed according to the specs of the Master Car Builders.

MONITOR: The raised center portion of a car roof.

MOTOR CAR: A self propelled car as distinguished from a trail car.

MULTIPLE UNIT CONTROL: A term applied to a control system designed to control two or more cars from a single control cab.

NARAGANSETT CAR: An open car embodying a two step construction which permits car floor to be raised without additional step length and width.

PANTOGRAPH: A current collecting device for an overhead conductor consisting of a jointed diamond-shaped frame carrying a pan which is pressed upward against the overhead wire.

PILOT: A V shaped slanting fender mounted under the end of a car body in front of the trucks.

PONY AXLE: The axle of a single motor truck which does not carry the motor.

PULLMAN WINDOW: A form of window arranged in pairs and surmounted by a narrow fixed sash usually of art glass.

RADIAL DRAFT GEAR: A form of coupler designed to permit the outer end of the drawbar to move laterally with respect to the center line of the car body.

RADIAL TRUCK: A long wheel base truck in which the axles are not confined to an exactly parallel position, but are allowed a slight end movement to permit them to assume a radial position when passing around sharp curves.

RESEVOIR: A steel tank for holding compressed air to operate the air brakes. Indicated as Main, or Auxiliary.

RHEOSTAT: A grid of iron resistance strips mounted under the car body and used to regulate the flow of current to the motor.

RUNNING BOARD: A folding step extending along the side of an open car.

SEMI-CONVERTABLE CAR: A cross seat closed car with entrance and exit platforms constructed so the upper and lower sashes can be dropped in pockets or removed for summer service.

SHEATHING: The narrow vertical matched boards forming the outside surface of a car below the windows.

SHORT WHEELBASE TRUCK: A motor truck in which the axles are placed close to the bolster and the motors are hung outside.

SIDE BEARINGS: Bearing plates mounted on the body and truck bolsters near their ends to prevent the car body from rocking.

SIDE SILL: An outside longitudinal side member of a car body underframe.

SINGLE END CAR: A car designed to operate always in the same direction.

SLEET CUTTER: A forked scraper attached to a trolley to remove ice from wire.

SPLASH PLATE: A board or plate dropped from the underframe of the car body to protect the electrical equipment.

TAIL LAMP: A lamp carried on the rear end of a car as a warning signal to following cars. Red light to rear, green to side.

THIRD RAIL SHOE: A flat iron plate hinged so it can move vertically and attached to the outside of a car truck so as to bear on a third rail located outside the track.

TRIPLE VALVE: A valve under each car in a train connecting the brake pipe to the air resevoirs, the brake cylinder and brake valves.

TROLLEY: The complete device including the spring base, pole, harp and wheel which is mounted on the roof of the car, and by means of which current is collected from an overhead trolley wire.

TROLLEY BOARD: One or more long boards nailed along the center of the car roof and forming a support for the trolley.

TROLLEY CATCHES: A device designed to arrest the upward motion of a trolley pole when the wheel leaves the wire.

TROLLEY HOOK: An iron hook on the roof of a car under which the trolley pole can be swung to hold it down when not in use.

TROLLEY RETRIEVER: A device for automatically pulling down the trolley pole, close to the roof when the wheel leaves the trolley wire.

TRUCK BOLSTER: The central cross member of a double truck which transmits the load from the body bolster to the truck frame.

TRUCK SIDE FRAME: The rigid truss, girder or forging forming the side of a truck frame.

UNDERFRAME: The framework in the bottom of a car body on which the floor is laid. It is made up of longitudinal sills, end sills and cross members.

VENTILATOR: An opening through which fresh air is admitted or foul air exhausted from a car interior.

VESTIBULE: An enclosed platform on the end of a car.

WHEEL FLANGE: The raised inner edge of the periphery of a wheel which projects below the top of the rail and holds the wheel on the track.

WHEEL TREAD: The surface of the periphery of a wheel which rolls on top of track.

www.ingramcontent.com/pod-product-compliance
Lightning Source LLC
Chambersburg PA
CBHW030518100426
42813CB00001B/83